THE GHURID PORTAL

THE GHURID PORTAL
of
the Friday Mosque
of Herat, Afghanistan

Conservation of a historic monument

ERIK HANSEN
ABDUL WASAY NAJIMI
&
CLAUS CHRISTENSEN

Photos by
KICKAN HANSEN

Aarhus University Press |

THE GHURID PORTAL
OF THE FRIDAY MOSQUE OF HERAT, AFGHANISTAN
Conservation of a historic monument

Typeset by Jørgen Sparre
Cover design by Jørgen Sparre
Printed in Denmark by Zeuner Grafisk 2015

ISBN 978 87 7124 913 2

Aarhus University Press
Langelandsgade 177
DK-8200 Aarhus N
Denmark
www.unipress.dk

INTERNATIONAL DISTRIBUTORS:

Gazelle Book Services Ltd.
White Cross Mills
Hightown, Lancaster, LA1 4XS
United Kingdom
www.gazellebookservices.co.uk

ISD
70 Enterprise Drive
Bristol, CT 06010
USA
www.isdistribution.com

Published with the financial support of VELUX FONDEN
and from the late Kickan Hansen

CONTENTS

DEDICATED TO HERITAGE CONSERVATION SPECIALISTS
HAVING WORKED IN AFGHANISTAN

Acknowledgement

The authors would like to thank Architect Flemming Aalund for his reading and comments on the first drafts of the manuscript. Thanks also goes to Hamayoun Ahamadi and Ayamuldin Ajmal, staff of the department of Herat monuments, for their quick responses to our queries.

PREFACE

The monumental Ghurid portal described in this book is a remaining of the original architecture and decorative art-work of the Ghurids in the late 12th century; it is also a Ghurid monument bearing restoration work by the Timurid rulers and artisans of Herat in the 15th century, therefore unique of its kind.

Another very important issue, looked at within this book, is the relevance of strategy and methodology in conservation undertaken exactly 50 years ago, evaluated against the various UNESCO conventions and ICOMOS charters available today: Authenticity, integrity, sustainability and durability of the preservation work.

The potential readership is envisioned to be students, architects, art historians and academics interested or engaged with research, restoration and teaching of architectural conservation of historical buildings in the Islamic world.

This book is organized into ten chapters. The first chapter illustrates the historical setting, geography and history of the Ghurid dynasty and their architecture. Chapter two describes the history of the construction and architecture of the Friday Mosque of Herat. Chapter three and four describes the Ghurid portal and the renovation of the portal by the Timurids in the 15th century. Chapter five and six are accounts by Erik Hansen about his UNESCO assignment in Afghanistan in support of the National Museum. Chapter six is the central section of this publication, where the restoration work is described in detail so future generations can understand the changes done. Chapters seven to nine cover the Ghurid and Timurid wall decorations and traditional Afghan masonry. Chapter ten provides a brief account on the continued efforts made for the restoration of architectural monuments in Afghanistan, focused on the Herat and Ghur provinces. The Appendix provides an attempt of reconstruction of the original Ghurid portal. ▪

Abdul Wasay Najimi
Kabul, 2015

INTRODUCTION

The peace in May 1945 ended a period of suffering and destruction in many parts of the world. Now a new world with trust and peace among nations should be created. United Nations was founded in October 24, 1945; followed by establishment of the special agency UNESCO, United Nations Educational, Scientific and Cultural Organization in November 1946. This book is describing one of the many restoration projects which were done by UNESCO, the restoration of the Ghurid Portal on the Friday Mosque in Herat, Afghanistan.

Danish scholars became interested in Afghanistan studies in 1947, when the Danish explorer and writer Haslund Christensen organized an expedition to Central Asia (1947-53) to investigate and describe the kingdom of Afghanistan.

A team consisting of anthropologists, botanists, geographers, and zoologists would work during 1948 and 1949 in Afghanistan, from Nuristan in the east to Herat in the west. Haslund Christensen fell ill and consequently passed away on 13th September 1948. He was laid to rest in the Christian cemetery (the walled *gura qabristan*) north of Shirpoor in Kabul, the Afghan capital. His work as ethnographer was continued by Lennart Edelberg (friend of the authors), who participated in the 1948 expedition as a biologist, but also in the early 1950s undertook some of the ethnographic tasks that remained unresolved after Haslund-Christensen's death. On this expedition, Edelberg had with him the newly graduated ethnographer Klaus Ferdinand and photographer Peter Rasmussen as well as an afghan student, A. A. Motamedi.

Edelberg travelled again in 1964 and 1970. He later presented two important publications on the community and architecture of Nuristan (1979 and 1984). Klaus Ferdinand continued to work in Afghanistan through Moesgaard Museum of Aarhus University, Denmark, and he supported three Danish students of anthropology/ethnography to having field work in Afghanistan in 1970s: Asger Christensen, Asta Olsen and Gorm Pedersen, who later worked in rehabilitation programmes through the Danish organization DACAAR in different periods between 1988 to 2009.

The above mentioned Dr. Motamedi later became the director of Kabul Museum, where he employed the French architect Alexandré Lezine to restore the Buddhist monastery in Guldara near Kabul under UNESCO premises in 1962.

1964 was by UNESCO declared to be the "Year of the Historic Monuments" which was marked by a large, international conference in Venice.

The first Afghan restoration project was started the same year: The Ghurid Portal on the Friday Mosque of Herat. Five young afghans were hired as restoration technicians with the Danish architect Erik Hansen as advisor. The work continued and was finalized in 1965. This was also the end of Erik Hansen's contract with UNESCO, but as a teacher in restoration at The Royal Danish Academy of

Fine Arts he had the opportunity during the following years to arrange one year courses in building documentation for each of the five technicians in Copenhagen.

At the same time DANIDA, Danish International Development Agency in cooperation with UNESCO made an agreement with the Afghanistan government to send architects who could lead restoration projects in Afghanistan: Johannes Hertz worked on the stabilization of the main iwan of Khwaja Abdullah Ansari complex in Herat (1967-68); Gilbert Jespersen worked on a project of diverting surface water from the Bamiyan Buddha cliff (1968-70) and Flemming Aalund worked on restoration of the Herat Citadel and the minaret site of the Madrassah of Sultan Hussain Baiqara in 1977-78.

Inspired by a film shown by Johannes Hertz from an iron foundry in Herat and through contact with Sultan Fayaz, one of the five Afghan technicians studying in Denmark, a Danish student of engineering, Claus Christensen started a development project in cooperation with a local group of foundry men in Herat. Later, he also came in contact with Abdul Wasay Najimi, one of the two architects graduated from Kabul University, who were granted a supplementary education in restoration in Copenhagen 1978. The second student was Masum Azizi.

Before they could finish their education Soviet Union invaded Afghanistan and they realized, that it would not be safe for them to return.

Masum could find refuge with family in USA, but Najimi stayed on in Denmark, and extended his study with a PhD in Architecture. As a Danish citizen he worked for several international NGOs in Pakistan and in Afghanistan including DACAAR in Herat from 1993 to 1995.

During this period he also traveled together with Bernt Glatzer to Shah-i-Mashhad and was visited by Claus Christensen, who returned to Herat for the first time after the Soviet invasion. Claus Christensen returned to Herat in 2002 and together with Najimi visited the minaret in Jam.

Lately as conservation architect through Aga Khan Trust for Culture (AKTC) Najimi was involved in projects in Herat in 2005-09 and he continues his work with AKTC up to now with restoration projects in Kabul and other places in Afghanistan.

During all these years the three authors had maintained their friendly and professional connections. So it happened that when meeting in Copenhagen in summer 2012 the authors agreed that the documentation from 1964, notes and drawings by Erik Hansen and photographs by his late wife, Kickan Hansen on the restoration of the Ghurid portal of Herat Friday mosque ought to be published. All photographs in this book are taken by Kickan Hansen in 1964 unless otherwise noted.

In a combined effort and thanks to modern technology within graphics and communication they have managed to produce this book despite Erik Hansen's age (88) and despite the fact that Najimi lives and works in Kabul, and only occasionally visits Denmark.

The authors hope that the reader will enjoy this book not only for its professional contents but also as a way of looking backwards to a time of prosperity in Afghanistan 50 years ago. ▪

Erik Hansen, A.W. Najimi and Claus Christensen
Copenhagen, 2015

Figure 1.1: The minaret of Jam in the Ghurid 12th century capital, Firuzkoh.

CHAPTER 1

THE GHURID DYNASTY IN AFGHANISTAN

MAKING HERAT THE CAPITAL

Being originally chiefs of the mountain tribes in the central-west region of today's Afghanistan, the Ghurids rose to power at Ghur (Gharistan / Gharjistan /Ghurat) a small isolated area located in the mountainous vastness between the Ghaznavid Empire at east and the Seljukids at west, in the 12th century. The area was so remote that its people were only converted to Islam after Sultan Mahmud of Ghazni raided the region in 11th century, and left teachers to educate the inhabitants and tribes there in the precepts of Islam. The Ghurids had been administratively bound to the Ghaznavids and Seljukids for about 150 years. Beginning in the mid-12th century, Ghur claimed its independence from the Ghaznavid Empire.

The Ghurid dynasty ruled over the territory making parts of modern day Afghanistan, Iran, Pakistan and north India for about 65 years (from 1150 to 1212 A.D). Firuzkoh, a hillside town on the bank of Hari Rud (river) in Ghur, was the first capital of the Ghurids. The Ghurid sultans, especially the two brothers Ghyath-ul-din and Muez-ul-din, ruled the vast territory earlier ruled by the Ghaznavids. Herat became the main capital town in the late 12th century while Ghazni and Lahore remained as the additional capitals in control of the eastern territories.

The first known ruler of the Ghurids was *Malik* Izz-ul-Din Husayn who became the *Amir* of Ghur in 1099 and who paid tribute to the Seljuq Sultan Sanjar (r. 1096-1157 AD) at Merv.

Qutb-ul-din Mohammad ibn Sam, the second son of Izz-ul-din, on inheriting his power built the fortification of Firuzkoh. Then his brother Baha-ul-din Hussain ibn Sam came to complete the works in Ferozkoh; he assumed power in 1149. After his death in Kaydan, a place near Gizab in today's Uruzghan Province, his brother, Sultan Alla-ul-din Hussain ibn Hussain ibn Sam assumed the power. Alla-ul-din Hussain took revenge and moved towards Ghazni, destroying and burning the city. He also imprisoned in a fort in Ajristan, a territory between Ghazni and Ferozkoh, his nephews Ghyath-ul-din and Muez-ul-din (sons of Baha-ul-din and the daughter of Malik Fakhr-ul-din of Kaydan), to keep them away from access to the seat of power.

Once the Seljuqs in the north-eastern Khorasan fell and the Ghaznavids became weak in Ghazni, the Ghurids resumed control claiming all of the territory previously administered by the Ghaznavids, at north in the lower-lands of Murghab valley, at west (Herat) and at south (Bust and Dawer) [lower and upper Helmand valley]. After the death of the tough and rude Sultan Alla-ul-din Hussain (*Jahansuz*) [the world burner] his son Sultan Saif-ul-din inherited the power in 1156. He released his cousins Ghyath-ul-din and Muez-ul-din and granted them full freedom. A young sultan, he was just and fair. He returned properties back to people, what his father had confiscated earlier (Abbas, 1971).

Map 1: The provinces of Ghur, Herat and Badghis.

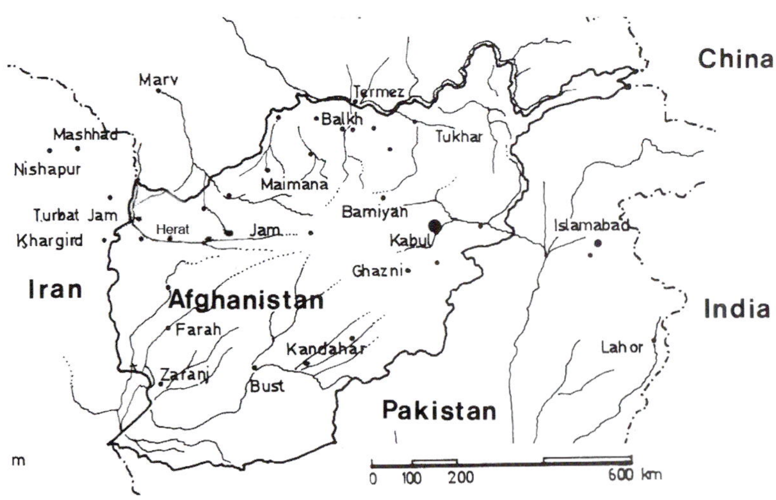

Map 2: Afghanistan in the region.

To some accounts, the site of Shah-i-Mashhad is attributed to the place where Sultan Saif-ul-din was buried in 1162-63. On that occasion, Sultan Saif-ul-din crossed the territory of Qādes (a district of Ghur), then a district of Merv (today's Turkmenistan), and moved for building a front of defence against and defeated the battle by Ghūz rulers. During the battle, however, the Sultan was killed by one of his generals, Abul-Abass Shish, who was taking revenge of his brother Darmish ibn Shish, a warrior who had earlier died being wounded by an arrow shot by Sultan Saif-ul-din in the fort of Firuzkoh (Jawzjani, 1864).

Sultan Ghyath-ul-din (cousin and brother in-law of sultan Saif-ul-din) took over the throne in 1163. The Sultan and his brother Muez-ul-din (later also known as Shahab-ul-din) returning from Bamiyan, where he served their uncle Malik Fakhr-ul-din, established a vast kingdom from east of the present Iran to northern India.

Sultan Ghyath-ul-din was a popular ruler. He was known as *Sultan Abul-Fat'ha Ghyath-ul-din Mohammad ibn Sam*. He was married to Jawhar Malik daughter of his uncle Sultan Alla-ul-din *Jahansuz* (and sister of Sultan Saif-ul-din). With this alliance he managed to add more territory to his rule. He took control of Herat in 1175 and Merv in 1192. It is relevant that the Queen Jawhar Malik sponsored the construction of Shah-i-Mashhad in commemoration to her brother's Martyrdom. Sultan Ghyath-ul-din died in Herat in 1202 (Jawzjani, 1864). His daughter Mah-Malik and his son Ghyath-ul-din Mahmud were two important personalities after him. Mah-Malik never got married and spent her life as a religious devotee and pious women having memorized the Quran (Jawzjani, 1864). Her brother Ghyath-ul-din Mahmud ruled over Bust, Farah and south-west parts of the Ghurid territory until he inherited the throne and came to Firuzkoh in 1205, perhaps also to complete the work on the minaret of Jam. Sultan Ghyath-ul-din Mahmud (son of sultan Ghyath-ul-din bin Sam) was killed in 1210, but was taken to Herat for burial in Gazargah. (Jawzjani, 1864; Abbas, 1971).

Important rulers of the Ghurid dynasty

Title	Name	Reign	Territory
Malik / Amir	Izz-ul-din	1099-	Ghur
Malik / Amir	Qutb-ul-din Mohammed s/o Izz-ul-din	?	Ghur
Malik	Baha-ul-din Hussain s/o Sam	1149	Ghur - Firuzkoh
Amir / Sultan	Alla-ul-din s/o Hussian/ Sam	1152	Ghur and Ghazni
Malik/ Abul-Muluk	Saif-ul-din Muhammad bin Hussain	1161-1163	Firuzkoh, Murghab Valley
Sultan Abul-Fateh	Ghyath-ul-din Muhammad son of Baha-ul-din bin Sām – the victorious	1163-1203	Ghazni to Persia and Herat as the capital
Sultan Shahāb-ul-din	Muez-ul-din Muhammad bin Sām	1203-1206	East to north India
Malik	Mahmud bin Ghiyath-ul-din Muhammad bin Sām	Firuzkuh 1206-1212	Ghor, Herat, Sistan and eastern Khorasan
Malik	Jalal-ud-din Ali bin Sām	Bamiyan 1206-1215	Takharistan, Badakhshan, Shughnan,

Figure 1.2: The minaret of Sultan Masud 3rd (1099-1114) in Ghazni.

ARCHITECTURE OF THE GHURIDS

Architectural style, construction technology and decorative techniques have travelled together with the masons and skilled labourers when they were seeking work in other territories. The building material would obviously be that found locally but the usage could be influenced by the masons coming from outside.

Geometric designs in brick work and knotted masonry was something the Ghurids inherited from the Ghaznavid period, as observed on the minaret of Masud 3rd in Ghazni built between 1099 and 1114, and of the minaret of Bahram Shah, built between 1118 and 1152 (figures 1.2 and 1.3). Structures

Figure 1.3: The minaret of Bahram Shah (1118-1152) in Ghazni.

remaining of the Ghurid period are easily identified by the style of construction, but also the typical kufic inscriptions that bear name of the Sultans and patrons of the constructions. All Ghurid structures in Shah-i-Mashhad, Chesht, Jam and Herat have such inscriptions and most bear the name of Sultan Ghyath-ul-din.

The Ghurid architecture had massive walls, arches and domes around a courtyard. The main façades were decorated with brick and terracotta laid in geometric patterns displaying kufic inscriptions. Interiors of the Ghurid buildings were plastered with gypsum and clay with decorative elements and inscriptions made in gypsum work, often carved out.

The Ghurid architecture is artistically best exemplified by the constructions in Shah-i-Mashhad, Jam, Chesht, and the Friday Mosque of Herat.

Figure 1.4: The Ghurid madrassa of Shah-i-Mashhad. Photo: B. Glatzer, 1971.

The first three buildings are described briefly in the following sections, as well as the now disappeared mausoleum of sultan Ghyath-ul-din bin Sam. The remaining chapters of this book concern the Friday Mosque of Herat with focus on the Ghurid Portal.

THE MADRASSA IN SHAH-I-MASHHAD

Shah-i-Mashhad is the name of an archaeological site and remaining of a 12th century Ghurid medressah building located on the bank of Murghab River, administratively in the district of Jawand of Ghur province in north-west Afghanistan close to the border of Turkmenistan. No roads leads to this place, which was discovered by scolars not before 1970 (meaning that the site was not know at the time when Erik Hansen worked in Herat). It was rich in architecture, design and religious decorative detail.

Inscriptions reveal that this education complex was inaugurated in 1175-76. This means that it is one of the oldest known remains of a madrassa.

While the majority of the construction in Shah-i-Mashhad was built from sun-dried bricks around a courtyard, important parts of the building were also constructed in baked brick masonry. Bricks were used both as construction material and as decorative elements. Intricate and carefully designed architectural and ornamental details were produced of thinner bricks and terracotta pieces where the proportions did derive of the brick size and dimensions (figures 7.3 and 7.18). Such works were

Figure 1.5: The Ghurid portal of the Shah-i-Mashhad. Photo: B. Glatzer, 1971.

Figure 1.6: Ruins of the madrassa in Chesht.

remarkable in Shah-i-Mashhad and Chesht buildings (next section). These are the best examples, in addition to what got lost of the Ghurid mausoleum in Herat, of the Ghurid style of decoration before glazing was used. Glazing is found at the Ghurid portal of the Friday Mosque of Herat and the minaret of Jam.

THE MADRASSA IN CHESHT

Chesht is a town situated on the northern bank of the Harirud River some 177 km east of Herat city. Here one also finds remains of the typical Ghurid work built in 1176 (Blair, 1985): A madrassa (education complex) with decorative brick masonry and inscriptions produced in bricks and unglazed terracotta (figures 7.4 and 9.1).

Ghurids were supporting education strongly and constructed attractive buildings for practice. It is said that there were more than seven major madrassa buildings in territories ruled by the Ghurids: Ghyasia in Herat (adjacent to the Friday Mosque) where Imam Fakhr-ul-din Razi was teaching; Ghur had the madrassa of Chesht and the Shah-i-Mashhad; Bamiyan had two madrassas that Seraj-ul-dine Menhaj was managing; Sistan had the Madrassa of Sar-i-hauz; Multan (modern Pakistan) had a madrassa known as Ferozi, managed by Menhaj-ul-seraj Jawzjani the author of Tabaqat-i-Naseri (Juzjani, 1864) and the city of Delhi had a madrassa named as Mu'ezi that was running until the era of Sultan Razia Begum (Nadem, 2010).

Figure 1.7: The glazed inscription on the minaret of Jam.

THE MINARET OF JAM

The Minaret of Jam is located in the Ghurid 12th century Ghurid capital, Firuzkoh, in a narrow valley at the site where the river Hari-rud merges with the river Jam. The minaret of Jam is surrounded by high mountains that reach up to 2400 m. The site is so remote that the presence of the historical minaret was first published in 1957. Many archaeologists and conservation specialists have travelled to this site since 1960s to study and suggest methods for protecting the base of the minaret from erosion and danger of flooding (figures 1.1 and 9.1). This place is today a UNESCO World Heritage Site in danger and well published.

Figure 1.8: Portal of the Ghurid Mausoleum in Herat in 1930s. Photo: Schroeder, 1935.

Having a diameter of 8 m and height of 63 m the minaret is built entirely of baked bricks. The outer shaft of the minaret, which has intricate decoration on bricks, stucco and glazed tiles (figures 1.7 and 7.5) consists of alternating bands of embossed kufic and naskhi calligraphy, verses from the Qur'an chapter 19th (the surat Maryam, relating to Mary, the mother of Jesus) and geometric patterns all made of brick elements. The glazed inscription scribes the name of the patron and date of its construction: that is Sultan Ghyath-ul-din in 1193-94. Perhaps this construction was the first site where the Ghurids used glazing for the brick inscription, as to some accounts its glazing is inferior to that of the Ghurid Portal of the Friday Mosque of Herat.

THE MAUSOLEUM OF SULTAN GHYATH-UL-DIN BIN SAM

The other monumental Ghurid construction was the mausoleum of Sultan Ghyath-ul-din, which either the Sultan erected in his lifetime or it was completed by his son sultan Mahmud Ghyath-ul-din in Herat. The mausoleum of Ghiyath-ul-Din was built to the north side of the mosque in 1203. (Juzjani, 1864). This building was then a separate unit with a dome construction. Although it was not originally a part of the Ghurid mosque, the southern side of the mausoleum had access to the mosque complex. The

Figure 1.9: Exterior wall decoration above the Portal of the Ghurid Mausoleum in 1930s.
The Kufic text says: *This holy tomb is …* هذا المشهد المبارک . Photo: Schroeder 1935.

interior wall decoration in the mausoleum resembled that of the mosque, patterned by the imitation of a look of exposed bricks, band of scripts and sacred names of God and the prophet Mohammad. As it was typical of Ghurid style, a horizontal stucco inscription encircled the interior of the chamber below the structure which supported the upper structural zone of transition (similar to the interiors in the domed chambers of Chesht and Shah-i-Mashhad).

These Ghurid structures, the mosque and the mausoleum of Ghyath-ul-din, which were badly damaged at the time of Chengiz Khan's destruction in Herat, were later restored by the Herat rulers of the Kart dynasty in 1306. They enlarged the mosque around the courtyard (limits as seen in the plan of 1942, figure 2.10) thus the mausoleum of Ghyath-ul-din bin Sam became attached to the new complex. The Timurids rulers of Herat restored the mosque and decorated its courtyard facades with glazed mosaic ornamentation.

In later Timurid repairs the exterior of the mosque also got transformed with tile decoration, but not the mausoleum. In 1833 the dome of the mausoleum collapsed (LAL 1834). The building was documented in Oscar van Niedermeyer's photographs of 1915. The Swiss architect, Ruedi Stuckert who spent time in Herat in 1942-46, published a detailed account about his observations of the Friday Mosque and the mausoleum. (Stuckert/Glatzer, 1980). The Swiss Foundation, Biblioteca-Afghanica, had Stuckert's original material published in 1994 *Rudolf Stuckert's memoir of Afghanistan from 1940 to 1946.*

Figure 1.10: The right side wall of the niche of the portal iwan of the Ghurid Mausoleum. The text is:

... شهنشاه الاعظم مالک رقاب الامم ...

Translation: ... *the greatest king of kings, who have followers of nations ...*

Photo: Robert Byron, 1933.

Figure 1.11: The portal like interior niche adjacent to the Friday Mosque. The wall plaster has a kufic inscription and decorative patterns of schematic inscriptions in square layouts. The inscription seen in soffit is:

... و المسلمين الظاهرفی العالم السلطان السلاطين ...

Translation: ... *and the muslims of the world, the sultan of sultans ...*

The kufic inscription is: ... هو الله اله لا الا هو و اله .

One inscription in the lower plaster is: محمد . Translation: *Mohammad*. Photo: R. Byron 1933.

Figure 1.12: The interior of the Mausoleum of Ghurid Sultan Ghyath-ul-din. Photo: Niedermayer, 1915.

Rich details of decorative brick masonry, prefabricated terracotta decorative elements and inscription monumentalized the portal and the main wall of the mausoleum. While some details and features resembled the work of the Ghurid portal of the Friday Mosque, it may not have had glazing on the inscription of its portal. This could indicate that the Ghurid portal of the Friday Mosque of Herat was planned and completed later than the Ghurid Mausoleum in Herat.

Unfortunately, nothing of the original decoration exist today. In modernization attempts and to widen the streets of Herat city after 1930s and remodelling of the exterior of the mosque after 1942-43, part of the mausoleums walls were damaged in 1944 (Frye, 1948). The remains of the mausoleum were demolished in 1950s for construction of the new mausoleum building that is part of the Friday Mosque complex of today (Hillenbrand, 2002).

Originally a large square structure, the new space of the mausoleum is an octagonal hall with circular niches on the interior walls. Externally, it is a three-sided projection on the northern wall of the mosque (figure 2.10), carved with three deep niches and crowned with two minarets all decorated in glazed tiles to give it an imitation of a post-Timurid look; it is situated on the axial line of one of the modern streets of Herat – *Jade Shemali Masjid Jami* – connecting the old city to the modern part of the town of Herat. ▪

Figure 2.1: The main iwan, *maqsura*, prayer hall of the Friday Mosque of Herat. Photo: Najimi, 2013.

CHAPTER 2

THE FRIDAY MOSQUE OF HERAT

THE HISTORY OF HERAT CITY

The history of Herat, especially of its Old City, has been one of repeated destruction and reconstruction. For its fertile land, the valley of Hari Rud has been the attraction for conquerors from west, north and east, who besieged the walled city of Herat, destroyed it and then rebuilt it. The citadel, one of the oldest structures in the city's historic centre, occupies a site that may have been inhabited as early as the 1st century B.C. according to recent excavations. The city of Herat was an important location on the Silk Road. Although Alexander the Great occupied Herat in 330 B.C., it is believed that the square layout of the Old City of Herat is from the early Islamic Period. According to Moqadasi and Ibn Saouk, Herat was already a large city with a citadel and four gates in 10th century (Zestovsky, 1949).

The Ghaznavid rulers of Herat made much civil and administrative construction here. In 1040, the Seljuqs attacked and destroyed the fortress of Herat, defeated the Ghaznavids, and ruled until 1175. Then, Herat administration affiliated itself with the Ghurid Sultans. Under the rule of Sultan Ghyath-ul-din, Herat remained as the capital for 40 years. Upon the death of Sultan Ghyath-ul-din, Herat became a target once again, and for a while it was controlled by the Khwarezm King (of the central Asia) who ruled from Merv.

Genghis Khan's forces attacked Herat in 1221 destroying the city causing the large building to fall to ruin. During a devastating earthquake in the middle of 13th century, the structure of the Friday Mosque got completely damaged and it was left to collapse. The new ruler of Herat Ghyath-ul-din Kart rebuilt the city and the mosque.

In 1381 Timur (Tamerlane) took Herat from the Karts, destroyed the city walls and plundered the city's treasure. His son, Shah Rukh, governor of Herat rebuilt the city and in companionship with his wife, Gawhar-shad, initiated revival of the lost cultural activities in Herat and made the city the centre of learning and culture. They made Herat their capital once they became King and Queen of the Timurid rule in mid 15th century.

After the decline of the Timurids, the Uzbek Shaibani Khan captured Herat in 1507. The Uzbeks of central Asia and the Safavids of Persia struggled for control of Herat until 1634, when Hasan Khan Shamlu (Safavid) became the governor of Herat.

The Hotaki Afghans struggled for Herat's independence in 1718. Herat became a province within the modern Afghanistan established by Ahmad Shah Abdali (Durani) in 1747. In the 19th century the descendants of King Timurshah Durani, and later on descendants of Amir Dost Mohammad Khan struggled for independent control of Herat, a process that continued until 1880. Herat became an integral part of the modern Afghanistan in 1885 when Amir Abdul-Rahman Khan became the King of Afghanistan.

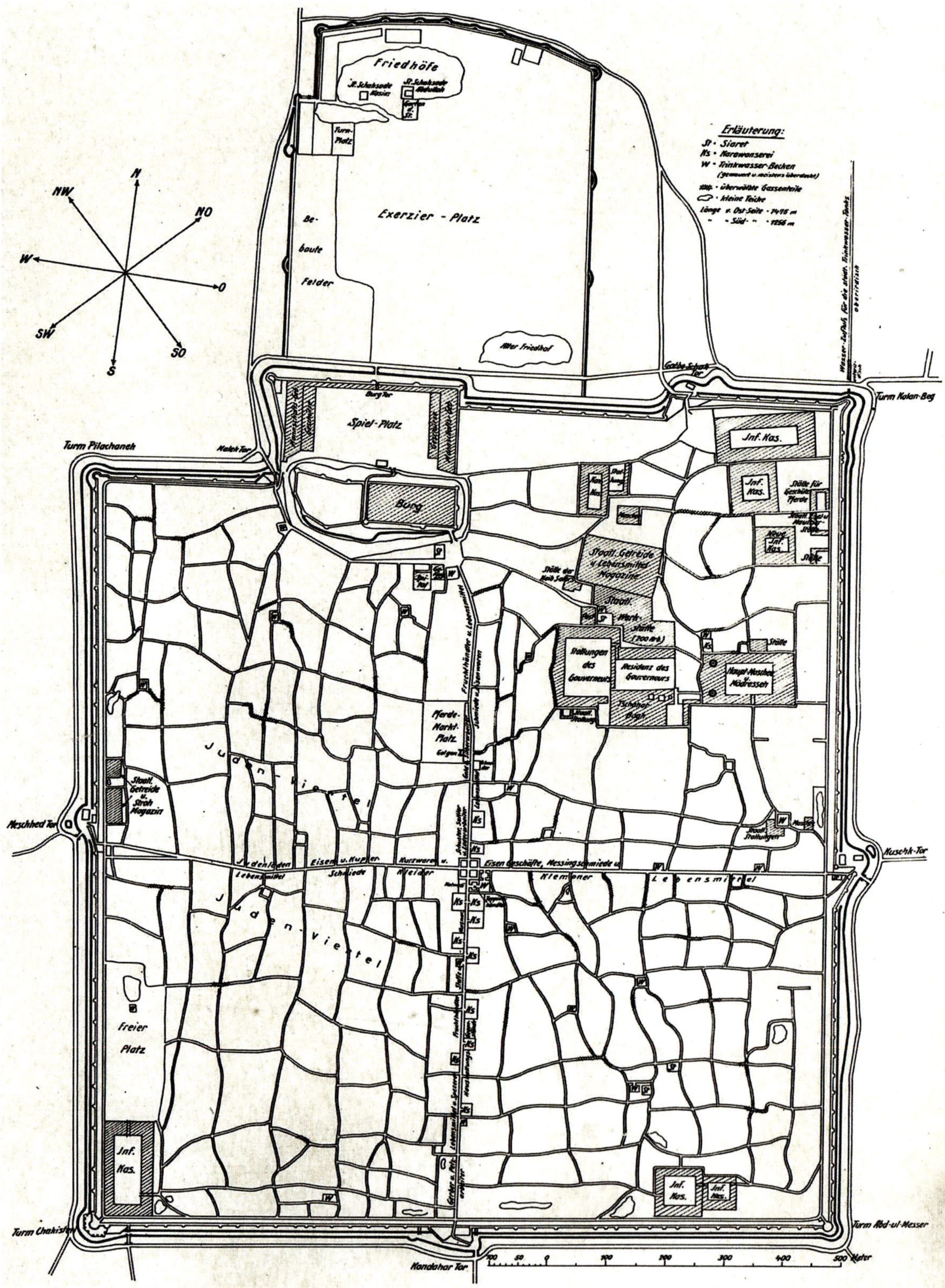

Figure 2.2: Map of the Historic city of Herat in 1915, sketched by O.v. Niedermayer. According to this sketch the Friday Mosque had Qibla (prayers orientation) at about 98 degrees west from magnetic North.

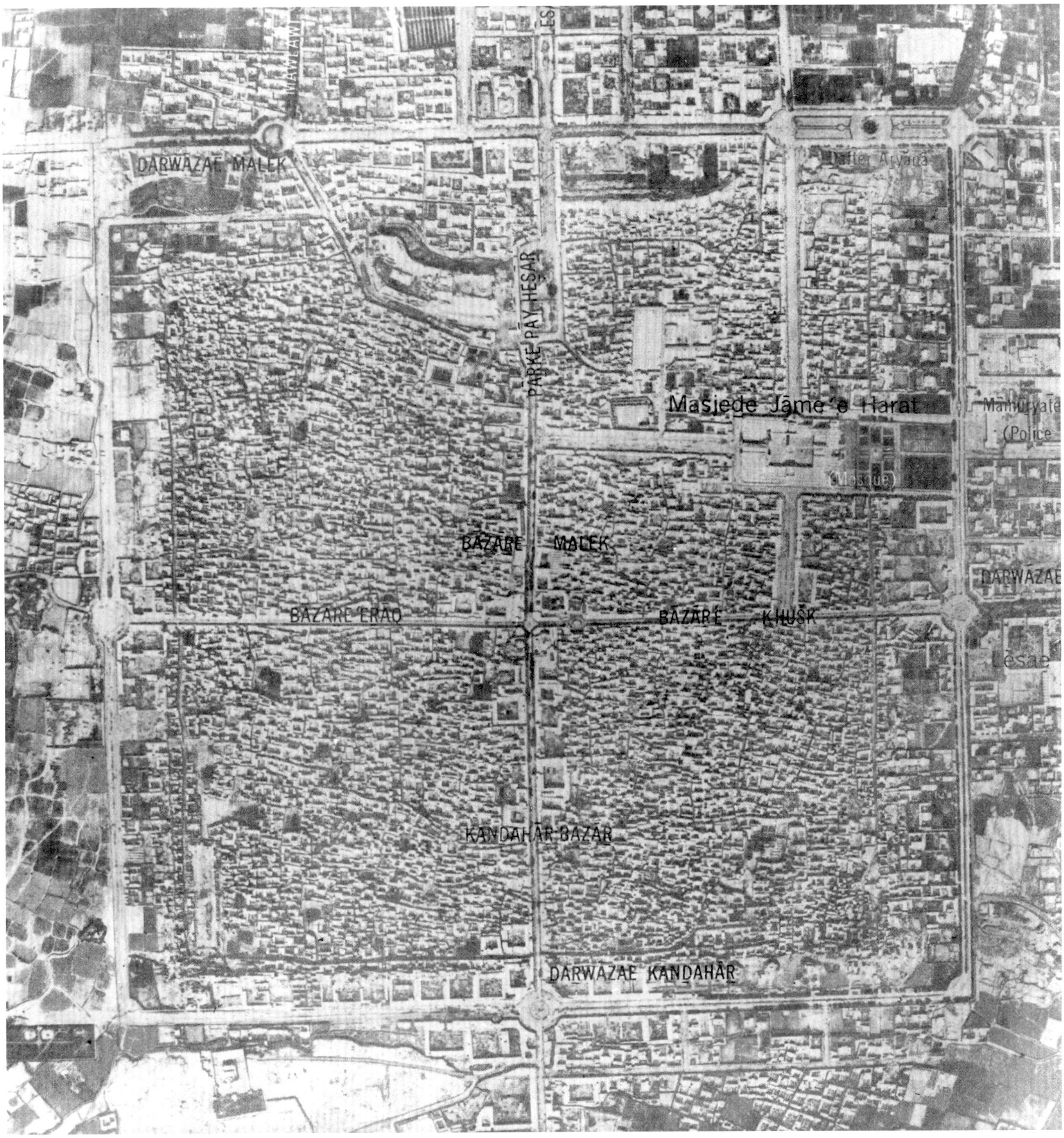

Figure 2.3: Aerial photograph of the Old city of Herat in 1960s. Source: Afghan cartographic department. New urban residential areas expanded to the north and east of the Old city, after the 1930s when the government intervened in the Old city, widened the streets of the four central Bazaars and realigned them with shops. Three new avenues cut through the Old city's north-east neighborhood to axially expose the Friday Mosque building – as in the Greco-roman cities.

Figure 2.4: Aerial view of the modern town of Herat. The major area of historic urban settlement is shaded. Photo: C. Christensen, November 2009.

SELECTION OF THE SITE FOR THE FRIDAY MOSQUE

The Friday Mosque is located at the North-East quarter of the Old City of Herat. This part known as Qutb-i-Chaq neighbourhood had been the administrative quarter of the city before establishment of the modern town (figure 2.2). It was believed that the site of the mosque was topographically higher then the rest of the old city terrain and was close to two of the five gates of the fortified city. According to Asfazari this site was easily supplied with water from the main channel, *joy-i-enjil*, feeding river water into the fortified city.

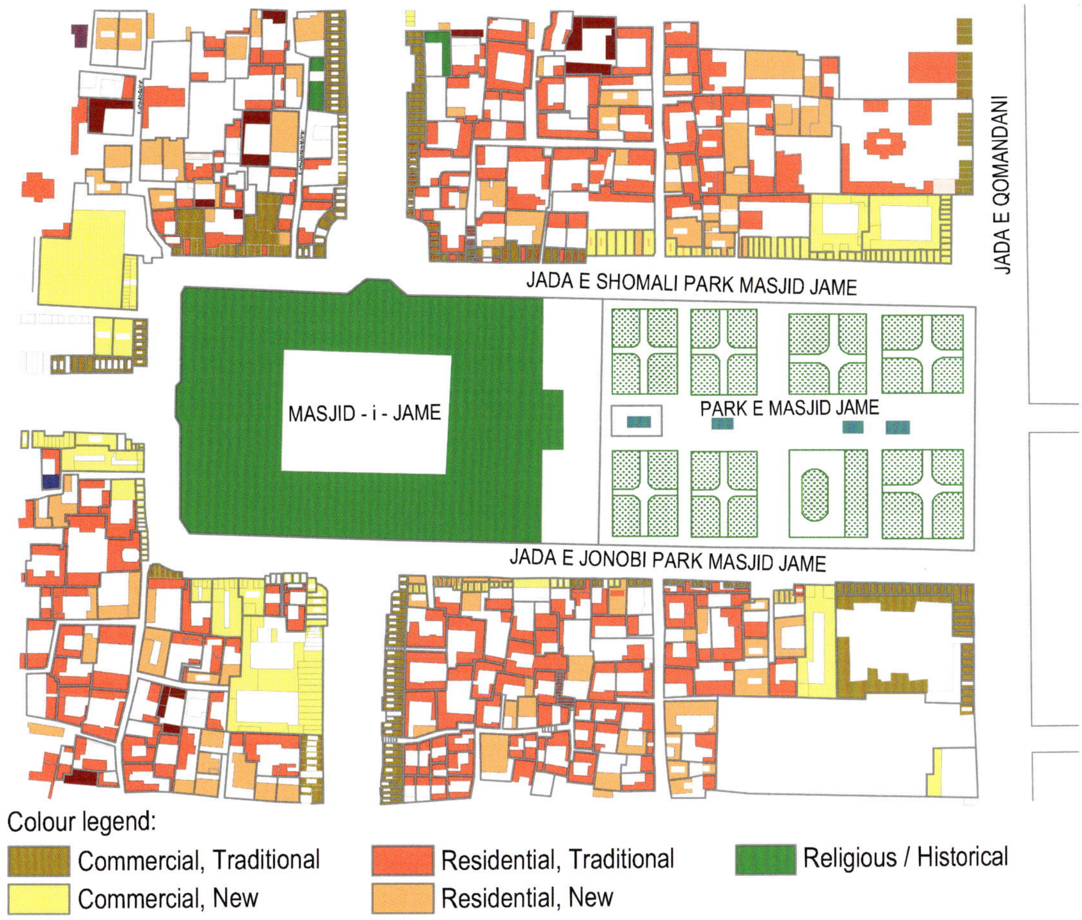

Figure 2.5: The Friday Mosque and its surroundings in the Old City of Herat today. From a survey of the old city houses by AKTC 2005-09. Scale 1:4000. Compare with figure 2.2.

CONSTRUCTION OF THE FIRST FRIDAY MOSQUES

It is said that a Zoroastrian temple existed inside the fortified city. Islam as a faith was introduced to people of Herat by Muslims lead by Ahnaf-ibn-Qais during the rule of the third Khalifa, Uthman, in 651.

The site of the Zoroastrian temple was refurbished into a mosque in the 7th century, and must have been expanded further especially by the Ghaznavids. The author of Hudūd-ul-Ālam (a 12th century geographic book in Persian) wrote that Herat had one of the best built Friday Mosques in 983. Sultan Mahmood of Ghazni and his grandson Sultan Masud 3rd (r. 975 to 1186) built many constructions including the Adnani palace in Herat.

Its solid structure was probably built by the Ghurids in 12th century. Its location near to the administrative quarter of the city of Herat has made the Friday Mosque an important venue. All rulers of Herat have taken pride in being patron to this mosque, its repair and maintenance for it being an important gathering place in both religious and socio-political coherence of the people of Herat, the city and the state government.

Figure 2.6: The Old city of Herat in 1915. The Ghurid Portal is visible at the upper right side of the picture. Photo: Niedermayer, 1915

Mosques have been the first schools of learning in the Islamic world; the Friday Mosque of Herat has also had the function of a *madrassa* (place of teaching, a school). As an important urban congregational facility in an Islamic City, *Masjid-i-Jami*, the Friday Mosque of Herat has been a focal point for Muslim worshipers of Herat city and its peripheries.

Originally, mosques in the region had some wooden elements in their structure. Columns and roofing beams were sometimes skilfully carved and ornamented. Findings of many stone column-bases in Herats Old City must have been the remains of such structures. The Friday Mosque of Karukh, a district east of Herat, still demonstrates this type of structure (figure 2.7).

The early Friday Mosque of Herat had wooden elements that caught fire from a thunderstorm and consequently got destroyed. Mir Khwand, the author of a book with the title *rawzat-ul-janat fi-al-awsaf-ul madinat-ul Herat* (paradise dwelling; in praise of the city of Herat) accounted that the incident happened on a Friday night in 1102. If it had happened during the daytime hundreds of worshipers could have been killed by the fall of the southern, western and northern sides of the structure. The people came to participate in the reconstruction of the mosque the next day. Herat has termites that damage wood, therefore most of the rebuild mosque has walls, arches and domes made of bricks.

Historian's account that the building of the mosque was smaller at that time. Today the Friday Mosque of Herat is the fourth largest historic urban mosque built in the Muslim world.

Figure 2.7: The wooden veranda of Karukh mosque, an example of the same wooden structure as in the old mosques of the Old City Herat. Photo: C. Christensen, 2005

ARCHITECTURE OF THE GHURID FRIDAY MOSQUE

It was mentioned in chapter one that the Ghurid Sultan Ghyath-ul-din Mohammad bin Sam, was patron of the construction of this grand mosque, after taking control of Herat in 1175. A famous scholar of 12th century Herat, Imam Fakhr-ul-din Razi was the spiritual initiator. The Sultan chose expansion of the site of the mosque, including the ruins of the previous building.

Inscriptions in the main iwan (*maqsura*), on the southern iwan and on the glazed inscription on the portals, document Sultan Ghyath-ul-din's direct involvement in the project and that it was completed in 1200-01 (see Chapter 6).

Juzjani, author of Tabaqat-i-Naseri (Juzjani, 1864) wrote that after the destruction of Firuzkoh mosque by flood Sultan Ghyath-ul-din, having secured Herat, ordered the transfer of the golden vase and chains used in Firuzkoh mosque to be traded in Herat city for funding the reconstruction of the Friday Mosque of Herat. While major parts of the construction were completed in Sultan's life time († 1202) minor works had to be continued by his son and successor Sultan Ghyath-ul-din Mahmood until its completion in 1210. A school (madrassa) known as Ghyathia was established in the northern part of the mosque. Famous scholars like Imam Fakhr Razi (b. 1149), Abdullah Ansari and Khwaja Mohammad Taki taught in this madrassa.

Figure 2.8: The Ghurid portal before restoration, enclosed by the new walls of the Friday Mosque inside the Old town of Herat, in 1964, seen from tower of the eastern modern portal of the Friday Mosque.

The exact plan of the building of the early Ghurid Friday Mosque is not explored through any archaeological studies. It is however clear that parts of the main iwan, southern iwan and the Ghurid portal are surviving evidence of the Ghurid mosque. Walls of the main iwan and parts of the mosque still bear historic plaster work and inscriptions similar to that of the mausoleum of Ghyath-ul-din (see chapters 1 and 7). This concludes that the plan of the Ghurid mosque was based on structures around an interior courtyard, though the constructed floor area was smaller than what we find today. Being the main mosque in the capital city, the structure was architecturally much more powerful. The main iwan of the Ghurid mosque reproduced the same stylistic model of covered space as that of the Sassanid Kasra Iwan in Ctesiphon. Therewith the three other iwans located on the cross-axis they functioned as teaching and gathering spaces for smaller audiences. The eastern iwan was larger than the two on the sides (northern and southern) which also had mihrabs allowing for smaller *jama'at* – daily congregations or group prayers.

The main direction for prayers (*qibla*) at any mosque should geographically align towards Mecca. Some scholars understood that Sultan Ghiyath-ul-din passively respected the original westerly orientation of the mosque that reflected the Hannafy tradition – one of the four Sunni schools of Islamic teachings (Golombek, 1983; Blair, 1985). The theological fact is: when difficult to calculate the exact direction towards Mecca then the orientation towards it is accepted as direction for *qibla*. From Afghanistan and further east it would be the west to orient to Mecca. From Herat the direction to *qibla* (Mecca) is 27.46° south of the geographical west (www.qiblafinder.com). Based on Google-earth's aerial photo the central axis of the mosque is more of East-West; According to Niedermayer's sketch of 1915 the mosque's qibla direction is 98° from the magnetic North i.e. 8° south of the exact west.

There was a pool of water in the courtyard. Water was supplied from North-west side and drained through the Ghurid portal at the south-east corner of the Friday Mosque.

WORK BY THE KART RULERS OF HERAT

During the occupation of Herat by Genghis khan forces in 1221, the city and the mosque were greatly damaged.

The Kart dynasty of Herat, also known as the Kartids, took control of the city in 1245, and from here they ruled over a large part of Khorasan during the 13th and 14th centuries.

Moiz-ul-din Kart, (r. 1331-1369) established a *khanaqa* (a space where *Sufi* devotees gather for group recitals). The Kart ruler, Ghyath-ul-din (r. 1370-1389) who was earlier subordinate to the Ghurid Sultan, repaired the structure and domes of the mosque while enlarging its floor plan. The author of *Khulasat-ul-Akhbar,* Khwand Amir, accounts that sultan Ghyath-ul-din Kart again established the madrassa (school) at the northern wing of the mosque complex and arranged for it a funding through *Waqf*: endowments from property revenues. The Kart ruler rebuilt the upper parts of the main *maqsura* iwan. Both of these Kart rulers are buried in the Ghurid mausoleum in Herat.

WORK BY THE TIMURID RULERS OF HERAT

During the Timurid empire Shah-Rukh being the governor of Herat (1385-1409) and then the head of the empire (1409-1447) made Herat his capital and undertook reconstruction of the city, bazaars and important buildings, including repair of the Friday Mosque. The Timurids kept the size of the mosque building and layout. They installed an ornamented marble mihrab inside the western wall of the mosque. They decorated the facades of the courtyards with mosaic tiles. Parts of this original decoration still remains on the south-west corner of the courtyard facades of the Friday Mosque (figure 8.2).

The governor Jalal-ul-din Firozshah under the rule of Timurid Shah-Rukh Mirza made good contribution to such works. The name of Shah Rukh was included in the glazed tile decoration on the courtyard façade of the western part of the Mosque (Goya Etemadi, 1964). Until 1493 the mosque had all the Ghurid, Kart and Timurid decorations, the Ghurid portal was not touched (Seljooki, 1964).

According to some accounts the main iwan got damaged due to structural settlement and environmental effects during the reign of Sultan Hussain Baiqara in the late 15th century. The sultan commissioned Amir Ali Sher Nawayee for repair and construction that started in spring, after the local New Year *nawroz* (21st March) in 1498-99. They replaced the damaged roofing and constructed stronger arches and vaults, and added flanking arcades on both sides at the roof level. The roof of the mosque was fixed with two brick layers and finished with final layers of mud and straw plaster. The work took two years and was completed in spring 1500.

The masons and tile masters worked for longer than one year to decorate the mosque with panels of glazed tile-composites in geometric and floral designs. At the main Mihrab a fine Minbar (preaching steps) produced in marble replaced the former wooden one. Later the Timurids also undertook repair, reconstruction and tile decoration of the Friday Mosque's external facades, including the Ghurid Portal in 1499.

Born in Herat, Ali Sher Nawayee (l. 1441-1501) was minister in the court of Sultan Hussain Baiqara (r. 1468-1504) and he devoted his efforts to keep Herat among the leading cultural and intellectual centres in the Muslim world.

WORK BY THE MUGHAL AND SAFAVID RULERS OF HERAT

The Mughals of India also renovated the Friday Mosque of Herat. When Shah Jahan (prince Khurram) after the fall of the Timurids was fighting for control of the region against the Uzbeks as Mohammad Khan Shaibani attacked the city of Herat in 1506-07. His forces under the command of the Safavid Quli-khan caused much damage to the city and the mosque. Unfortunately many of the decorations were damaged.

The Persian Shah Ismael Safavid recovered Herat and its related territories in 1510. The Mughals and Safavids remained friends with the Uzbeks. The Safavids struggled for Herat until 1634 when Hasan Khan Shamlu became the governor of Herat under them. He also built the covered water cistern of Charsuq in the old city. (Najimi, 1982).

WORK BY THE AFGHAN RULERS OF HERAT

The former frontal façade of the main iwan (*Maqsura*) dating from the Timurid period collapsed during the 18th century and parts of the Friday Mosque were destroyed and repaired in the 19th century. Yar Mohammad Alekozai (minister at the court of Kamran Sadozai after 1829 but autonomous after Kamran's assassination in 1842) undertook repairing the mosque in 1837. King of Afghanistan from 1863 to 1879 , Amir Sher Ali Khan also commissioned some repair works. Further repairs took place after 1885 when Amir Abdul Rahman Khan became the King of Afghanistan.

WORK IN THE 20TH CENTURY

Amir Habibullah commissioned some repairs in the Friday Mosque that took 5 years in the early 20th century. Governor of Herat under King Habibullah, Mohammad Qasem allocated funds of 200.000 Afghanis for major repairs in 1907. The work included raising and resurfacing the interior floor levels with burnt bricks.

Oscar Van Niedermayer, member of a German delegation to Afghanistan passing through Herat,

Figure 2.9: The courtyard and main prayer iwan of the Friday Mosque, before renovation of 1940-50. Photo: Niedermayer, 1916.

made photographic documentation of the Friday Mosque in 1914-15. He described it as one of the best constructions of Herat and similar in grandeur as the mosque of Ibn-Tulun of Egypt. His photograph showed that the Kufic inscription in plaster in the main iwan was still preserved and that the courtyard oriented facades that earlier were decorated by cut bricks and terracotta pieces (Ghurid) were then seen redecorated by glazed tiles (Timurid) and the mosque had five entrances. The repairs of 1913 survived until 1941.

The mosque was enclosed by nearby residential houses through which the winded narrow streets connected access to the gates of the mosque. In 1941 the well-off merchants of Herat raised funds for yet another repair and restoration work of the Friday Mosque to be undertaken. On behalf of the Afghan government during King Zahir Shah's reign, Herat Governor Abdullah Malikyar took upon the assignment and initiated comprehensive restoration in 1942-43. The Swiss architect Ruedi Stuckert was in town and was involved as consultant in the city's work.

The government's first move was to demolish the houses and structures attached to the mosque and provide free space around the mosque complex (figure 2.3). The second action was to decorate the exterior with tile works in traditional style of post Timurid patterns. About sixty young men worked full time for two years in the project.

According to Fekri Seljooki (2001) the building of the Ghyathia madrassa (Quranic school), near the mausoleum of Sultan Ghyath-ul-din bin Sam, was not repaired since 1907 (the rule of King Habibullah). This was renovated when the mosque complex was regularized at its Northern part in years 1940-49, as

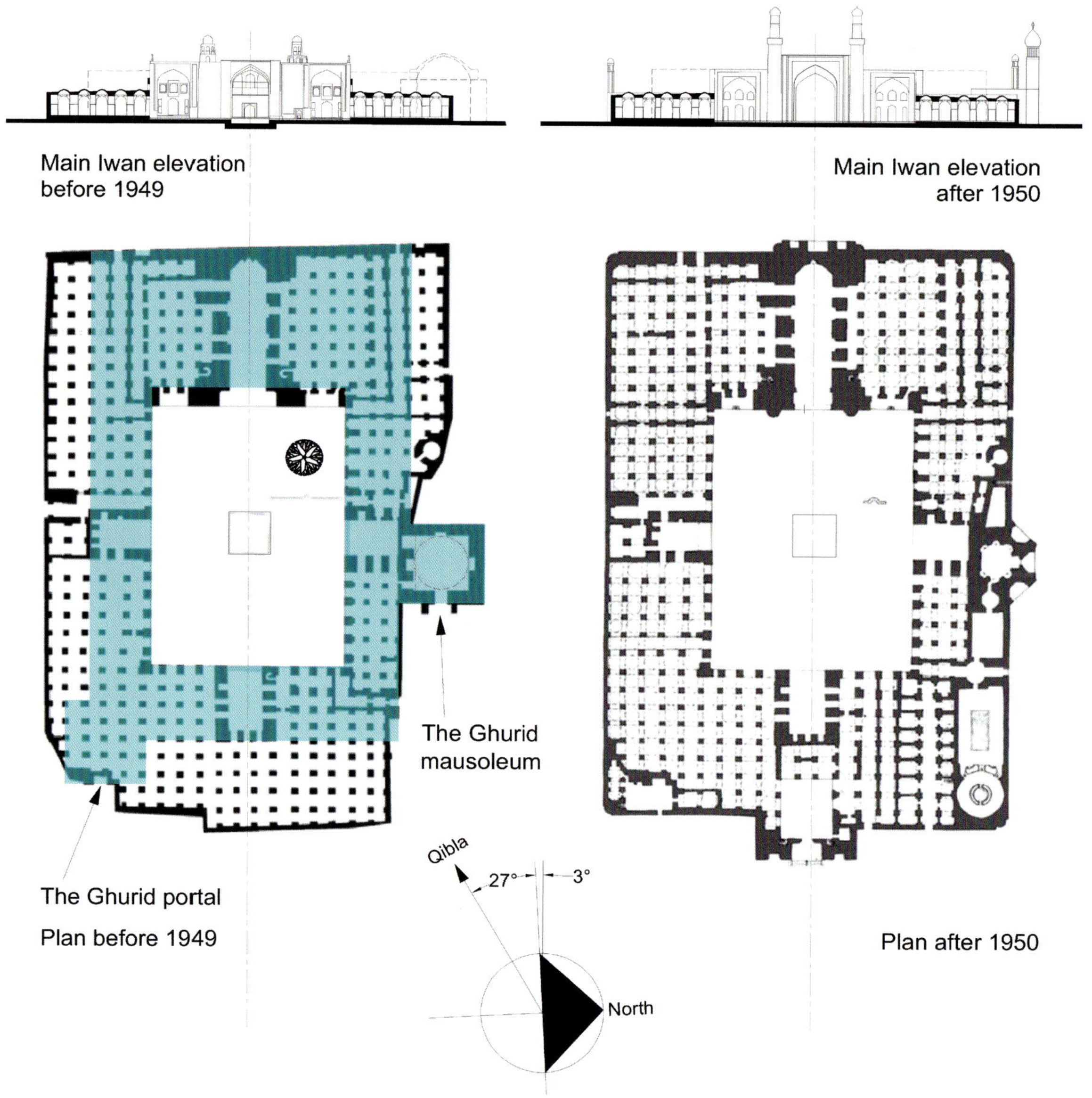

Figure 2.10: Comparative plans and main iwan elevations of the Friday Mosque, sketched by Najimi in 2013, after plans by Stuckert (1942), Samizay (1981) and AKTC (2007-08). Scale: 1:2000. The shaded area is assumed by the authors as part of the Ghurid Mosque before the Kart rulers enlarged its floor plan in the 13th century.

the madrassa was moved to the north-eastern wing of the complex. It has been known as Madrassa-i-Jamae Sharif (named after the Friday Mosque) with its own entrance from the east (the park).

The *maqsura* iwan that had structural damages was rebuilt through the renovation works of 1940s. A new front design was advised: The 45 meter deep iwan was made stronger and higher (20 metres from the floor level) flanked by two tall minarets springing from ground level and replacing the former stubs that earlier stood on top of the building. The base of the new minarets were so wide that half of the base projected into the courtyard. These minarets were raised to a height of 35 metres. Ten more minarets, additionally, were erected on the corners of the complex (Ghawas, 1982).

Talented masons and artists made up the professional team. Haji Mohammed Ismael muhandis led the repair and construction of the eastern iwan in 1936-44 (Zestovsky, 1949).

Figure 2.11: Congregation in the Friday Mosque in autumn of 1964. In colder seasons people tend to enjoy sun when praying outdoor and in the courtyard. Notice that few people are setting in the shade.

Others were Ghulam Haidar muhandis, Haji Juma Gul and Khwaja Jalal-ul-din Heravi. Abdul Rauf Fekri Seljooki and Ustad Mohammad Saed Mashal were designers of the patterns and tile decoration. Haji Mullah Abdullah Herawi, Mir Aqa Hussainee (who mastered *nastalique* style of inscription died 1953 at age 80) and Ustad Mohammad Ali Atar Herawi (who knew seven styles in calligraphy) were the calligraphers of the inscriptions produced in glazed tiles installed on the facades of the restored mosque (Ghawas, 1982).

All courtyard facades were completed with traditional patterns of decoration in glazing in seven colours. The plinth of all arcades were resurfaced with marble panels and the arcades got corners columns installed, which were made of marble in adaptation of the Timurid winded columns.

Perhaps damaged, the original tiled inscriptions bearing verses of the Quran and poems by Ansari, Jami, Saadi and Sanayee were replaced during the restoration/renovation by work of the contemporary

Figure 2.12: The tile decorated base of the minaret of the main iwan after renovation of the Friday Mosque in mid 20th century.

calligraphers Fikri Seljooki and Muhammad Ali Atar. New panels of verses of the Quran, written in *Thulth* style of calligraphy and Persian poetry in *nastalique* style, made part of the ornamentation. These works were initiated in 1943 and were finished by 1952.

The mausoleum of Sultan Ghyath-ul-din, which measured 45 by 45 metres externally (Zestovsky, 1949) was damaged and left roofless for years, was to be rebuilt. The original walls that enclosed a large square chamber of the mausoleum (12 by 12 m) were taken down and replaced by smaller mausoleum with an octagonal interior and facades in style with the rest of the exterior of the complex. At the north-east part of the complex, near the northern entrance, a new courtyard for storage space, facilities and ablution was added.

Overall, the mosque's multiple reconstructions and restoration programs left very little of the

Figure 2.13: A student is using the base of the new minaret as a seat, enjoying the winter sun.

authentic and original gypsum-carved (Ghurid) and glazed (Timurid) decoration exposed. A small portion of Timurid work is found at its south-western part of the courtyard facades.

The floor of the courtyard was repaved with burned bricks measuring 30 x 30 centimetres (figure 2.13). These allowed for quick drying floor after rain, as water drained and absorbed quicker. The floor was not hot in summer.

In 1956, a Mihrab produced of Rukham stone (Alabaster) from Helmand was donated by King Zahir Shah and was installed at the courtyard of the mosque, under supervision of Ustad Mashal (figure 2.17). This provided the worshipers with an open air congregation / prayer space; sunny space on a winter day and cooler on a summer evening. Fittings were installed on the courtyard side of the northern wing, to establish closed and warmer space for prayers in winter (Ghawas, 1982). Part of the

Figure. 2.14 (a, b): The main prayer iwan (looking to courtyard) and the side-archways of the iwan where the Ghurid inscription in Plaster supports the brick-work decorative vault above.

Figures 2.15 (a, b): The interior spaces and structure of the mosque with columns and domes.

previous madrasa attached to the Ghurid Mausoleum became a hall for *Fateha khana* (gathering to condolence the bereaved family men).

Externally, an additional iwan flanked by two minarets was completed at the western exterior of the mosque complex. The gate from the western side was closed, two gates from North, two from South and one from East provided access for worshipers entering the courtyard of the mosque. The eastern side of the mosque was also modified: An iwan and entrance port flanked by minarets was constructed behind the eastern large iwan (Tirard-Collet, 1998) (figure 2.16).

Figure 2.16 (a, b): Construction and decoration work on the minarets and exterior of the Friday Mosque in 1964. The channels in the old city still had water.

The campaign of reconstruction / renovation inaugurated in 1943 was gradually completed in 1973. In general one might say that this restoration program resulted in expansion of the mosque at its north-eastern section from a length of approximately 101 m to 121 meters. The new plan of the mosque was a result of correcting the irregularities in the exterior of the original mosque building. A grand park was established to the east of the Friday Mosque, replacing the previous street and space, including the eastern rampart of the fortified city wall.

RESTORATION OF THE GHURID PORTAL IN 1964

While work was still going on for completion of the remaining construction and minarets of the Friday Mosque of Herat (figure 2.16), the Ghurid portal was restored by Erik Hansen in 1964. This restoration work is described in chapter six.

DRAIN FROM ABLUTION POOL

An ablution pool was situated in the courtyard of the Friday Mosque (figure 2.9). Water was supplied into the mosque from its North-Western side (figure 2.16 b) and was drained in a channel through the Ghurid portal (figure 4.1). During the restauration in 1964 it was discovered that this channel created continuous moisture that had weakened the foundation.

The foundation was strengthened in 1964 with a masonry of baked bricks and a mortar of lime, ash and sand. In 1968 the local team of conservation responsible for the safeguarding of the mosque diverted the water channel to a new drain southwards; they preserved the structure of this historic channel but it is no longer used. The ablution pool was abandoned after the mid 1970s.

Figure 2.17: The courtyard half way paved with marble plates. Photo: C. Christensen, 1994.

THE NEW MANAGEMENT OF THE FRIDAY MOSQUE

During the conservation- and renovation works of the Friday Mosque the government established an endowment fund financing the future maintenance of the building and tile work of the mosque in a sustainable way. A two percent special tax on import and export through Herat custom was assigned. A committee chaired by Herat governor should manage the accounts. The tile workshop, as part of the complex, and masons having worked in the project remained the responsible maintenance team.

WORK IN 1977-78

The floor of the courtyard paved with square burnt bricks was wished to be repaired again. In 1974, they initiated resurfacing the courtyard with marble plates. People were mobilized and each Herati trader donated for the cost of 10 to 50 marble plates in size of a prayer mat (80cm x 120 cm). Lines between each row (of prayers line) were to be paved with darker and slender stones. This work remained incomplete in 1977, as it was also controversial.

In 1986-87, a native of Herat, governor Fazel Haq Khaliqyar financed, from endowment funds of the Friday Mosque, Ustad Mashal and his two pupils (Tawfiq Rahmani and Nasir Sawabi) to decorate in gypsum-work one of the mihrabs in the winter hall of the Friday Mosque. This work was completed in early 1993.

Figure 2.18: The eastern entrance to the Friday Mosque with minarets built in the 1960s. The wooden door was installed in 1994 for women to enter the Friday Mosque. Photo: C. Christensen, 2012.

Marble pavement of the courtyard resumed in 1992 and continued until the end of the decade. The outdoor alabaster mihrab was moved more into the central axis in 1996 when Taliban controlled Herat. The outcome of the marble floor has been a surface which perhaps is easy to clean and sweep, but it is also a disturbance to the outdoor worshipers: In summer the glare of the sun is reflected and blinding, and the stones become very hot. In winter the cold and slippery floor is uncomfortable for outdoor congregation and for walking barefoot.

WORK SINCE 2002

The roofs of the Friday Mosque got resurfaced, starting in 2002. They moved the thick layer of earth accumulated from many years of mud-plastering, which also provided insulation. Instead they plastered the top of the brick vaults and domes with a layer of cement plaster, which was topped by a layer of waterproofing alufoil – asphalt sheets, locally known as ISOGAM and comes from Iran. As a consequence, interior of domes of the mosque revealed accumulation of moisture. Perhaps the building lacked proper breathing, or lack of the thicker layer of soil on the roof allowed for condensation and moisture in the ceilings.

Through yet another maintenance work in 2004-05, the old plaster was peeled off in some walls and plastered anew, attempts were made to straighten the vertical surface of the otherwise slightly leaning walls of the main iwan. However, some of the Ghurid original wall plaster became visible and is now exposed in frames within the new plaster work.

Figure 2.19: West side of courtyard. Photo: Najimi, 2013.

Figure 2.20: East side of courtyard. Photo: C. Christensen, 2012.

Figure 2.21: The south-east corner of the Friday Mosque, where the Ghurid Portal is today inside the small courtyard behind the wall built in the 1950s. Photo: Najimi, 2013.

THE FRIDAY MOSQUE AT PRESENT

Today the Friday Mosque complex is a landmark of Herat city. The complex is 180 metres long, 120 metres wide occupying a total floor area of 21600 square metres. The constructed area covers 15500 square metres where the courtyard is 4879 square metres (82 metres by 59.5 metres) (Boostani, 2012). In addition to the four large iwans, the mosque has 460 domes and 444 pillars. Facades of the iwans have monumental inscriptions of verses from the Quran and poetry of famous religious scholars. There are 130 open and blank arches on the facades around the courtyard and externally. The complex today has 12 minarets from 17 meters to 36 meters height. The complex is also a touristic attraction in Herat (Ghawas, 1982). East of the Friday Mosque the park has been modernized in 2004.

While appreciating all the renovation of the Friday Mosque it is quite sad that the remains of the Ghurid mausoleum was lost in quest of a renovation. There was no law for the protection of the monuments and cultural heritage earlier than 2004.

Restoring a historic monument not only poses technical problems, but also aesthetic and historical issues that especially have been a complicated case in the monument of the Ghurid Portal. ▪

Figure 3.1: The restored facade of the Ghurid portal of the Friday Mosque of Herat, 1964.

CHAPTER 3

THE PORTAL OF THE GHURIDS

The portal was built by Ghurid Sultan Ghyath-ul-din as part of the Friday Mosque, when the general plan was designed for this large city mosque. This portal was not situated axially but at the south-east corner of the Friday mosque (see figure 2.8 and 2.10) because the portal was a major access into the mosque from the street east of the mosque. It runs parallel to the city's eastern rampart and is connected to the Khosh gate of the fortified city.

The height of the structure surveyed was actually 10.5 m but may have originally been some 2 m higher. The top of the Ghurid arch was 9.5 m above the ground.

The portal niche was an opening 445 cm wide. It had given access to the interior of the mosque, but now (1964) the entrance was closed by a brick wall. The exact date of abandoning this entrance is not remembered, but the Ghurid portal has been closed since long. The other gates were perhaps used more frequently.

The Ghurid portal remained as two monuments (Ghurid and Timurid) in one structure. The lower arch, below the Ghurid arch and vault are the remaining of restoration and stabilization work by the Timurids in the 15th century (See Chapter 4 and 6).

This structure was in severe degradation in 1964 and had to be restored.

THE SUBSTRUCTURE OF THE WALLS

Typical of the Ghurid portals, this construction was conceived as a projection of the main building. The actual projection could not be measured externally in 1964 as new constructions had been built near to it after 1950.

The structure at the base of the portal was a plain brick-construction 900 cm long, 270 cm deep and 160 cm high, comprising about 18 courses of masonry over the floor level, which seemed to be original (figure 3.2).

Above the substructure in the back-wall corners, we could see two solutions for the vertical continuation of the brick-masonry of the wall. It was the limits of the original opening or more probable a niche in which the doorway opened (figure 3.3 plan I and figure 6.13b).

THE FRONTAL FACADE

Two decorative masonry columns with an outer diameter of 44 cm, height of about four meters including their base and capital, flanked the front of the portal niche. The columns were decorated by terracotta elements, cast or cut to shape and sat in mortar forming a floral pattern winding around to the top. These columns were placed with their outside diameter aligned within the line of decorative

Figure 3.2: Right side of the portal with the decorative round corner column on substructure and the start of the Kufic inscription.

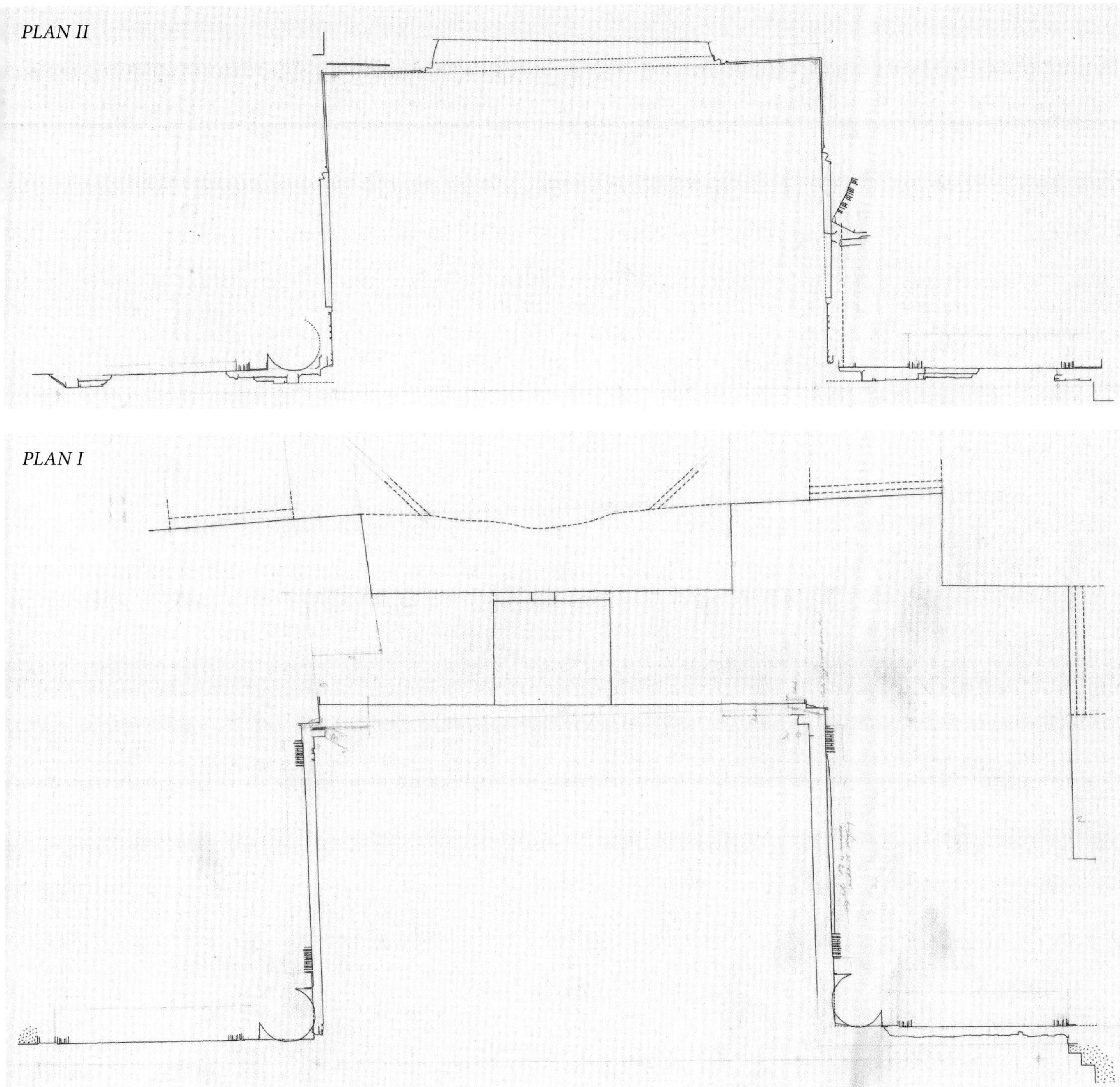

Figure 3.3: Measured drawings of plans at different height levels of the structure. Plan I: 4 m above ground level. Plan II: 5.4 m above ground level (top of decorative column). Scale: 1:50. Erik Hansen, 1964.
Note that the information in these plans indicate different levels i.e. the left side details shows plan under the section line while the details at right indicate the plan above the section line.

Figure 3.4: Detail of the masonry above the capital of the corner columns, left side.

surfaces of the walls. There was no space between the columns and the structure probably because the column was made of shaped bricks which were bonded with the bricks behind. A similar construction of the columns can be seen in Shah-i-Mashhad (figure 1.5) where the columns are deteriorated so the bricks can be seen.

Above the capital of the corner columns the building program had changed completely: 12 courses of brick panel (figures 3.4 and 3.5) maybe with space for an inscription on the sides of the bay, as we know them from e.g. Shah-i-Mashhad (figure 1.4).

We cannot know for sure because the position of the columns' upper capitals was the place where the original Ghurid masonry had been cut by the Timurids for making space to construct the base of a new vault.

Figure 3.5: Detail of the masonry above the capital of the corner columns, right side. A part of the Timurid side panel and the arch with Timurid decorations is also visible.

Higher up on the façade the two thick backgrounds of the columns were replaced with thinner work of masonry that was continued vertically higher, where the masonry began taking part in the upper and original Ghurid structure. Beside this support of the arch a list of shaped bricks framed the arch (figure 3.1).

The Ghurid arch was in type a pointed arch and its structural tip had been slightly under the edge of the disappeared horizontal band of the inscription above (see next section).

On the facade, the plane between the arch and the inscription was decorated in the form of bee-hive construction produced with terracotta elements sat in geometrical order (figures 3.1 and 7.7). In addition intricate work in thinner bricks and terracotta made the decoration that surrounded this monumental entrance.

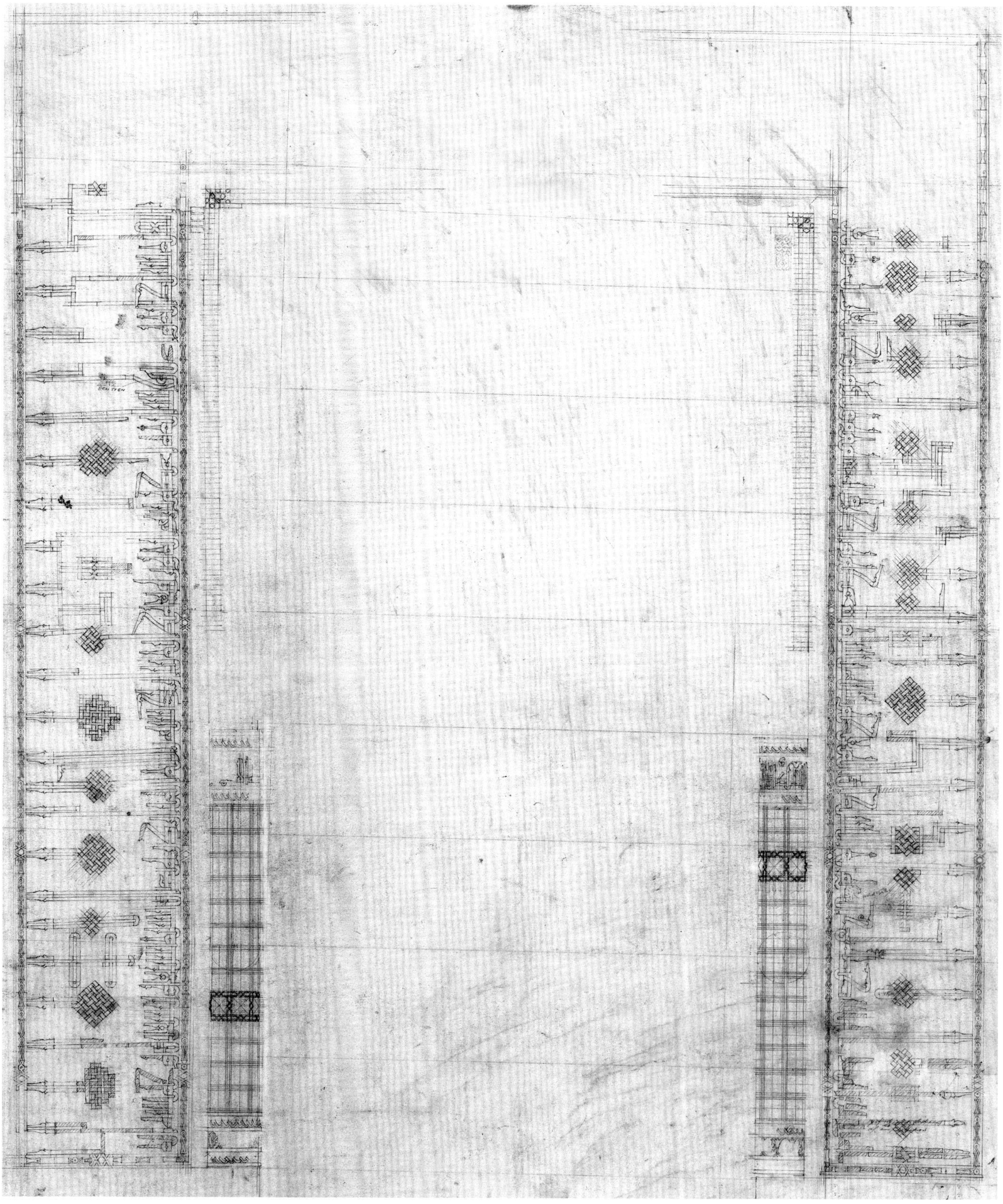

Figure 3.6: Measured drawing of the inscription. Scale: 1:20. Erik Hansen, 1964.

THE INSCRIPTION OF THE PORTAL

The richly decorated façade of the portal is dominated by the large inscription-band with letters of Kufic style in turquoise-blue glazed ceramics.

The inscription starts and ends just above the substructure masonry. The reading of the inscription begins from the bottom right (the northern pillar) going upwards until it disappears. It has probably continued higher and turned left above the arch. In 1964, having observed a few remaining fragments of the uppermost of this frame, we were able to estimate the total height of the inscription panel (also see Appendix). On the left (the southern pillar) the text continues from the top downward to the substructure.

The two vertical inscription-bands were preserved during the works of restoration in 1964.

The Arabic text recorded was:

Right side:

امرببناء هذه المسجد من الخاص ماله السلطان المعظم، شهنشاه الاعظم،
مالک رقاب الامم مولی ملوک العرب و العجم ...

Left side:

[خلد] الله سلطانه و اعلی شانه و اعظم برهانه و رفع مکانه تبارک [فی]
شهرالله المبارک رمضان سنه سبع و تسعین و خمس مائه

The inscription documented that the mosque was built by Sultan Ghyath-ul-din, with his own resources and that it was completed in the month of Ramadhan in year 1200 (597 AH) (See also chapter 6).

The left band was 156 cm wide while the right band was only 144 cm. The distance between them was 567 cm. The preserved height was 860 cm and the whole width of the façade (from outside to outside of the inscription) was 867 cm.

The total length of the inscription including the lost sections at the top of the inscription was 25.9 m. The bottom of the letters are at the bay side of the portal.

The letters are framed on both sides by a neutral 12 cm wide brick border (figure 3.4) and a decorative band. This band (figure 3.8 left side) is composed of a chain of keyhole-shapes followed by a floral pattern crowning the twisted square-knots of the tails of the letters of the inscription (figure 7.22). This band made of formed and glazed bricks are sitting on a background of unglazed floral-decoration made of palmettos with a mark of glaze on them.

What is particularly remarkable is the tree-dimensional execution of these designs that are implemented in three levels of depth: first the glazed inscription and its extensive ornaments, behind

Figure 3.7: The southern side of the great inscription and related decorative elements.

the series of floral-leaf palmettos background and then the plaster bed where all the decorative bricks are set in a layer of gypsum-sand mortar.

The bricks used for making the inscription measured about 22 cm in length while they were 3.5 to 3.7 cm in thickness. The inscription was projected about 3.6 cm from the palmettos decorative elements that itself was sat in gypsum bed setting about 5.0 cm behind. The knots were made of glazed projections of 7.5 by 3.3 cm and with same length as the bricks (22 cm). (See also chapter 7).

Figure 3.8: Detail of the elements making the ornamental framing and the monumental inscription.

THE SIDE PANELS

The side panels sitting on North and South facing walls of the niche (figures 3.9-3.12) were covered with a geometrical pattern disposed in a square system of prefabricated baked bricks (terracotta), 2.2 cm thick, elements shaped to purpose.

The surface of the mortar used for this masonry lay 4-5 cm deeper than the front of the decoration bricks.

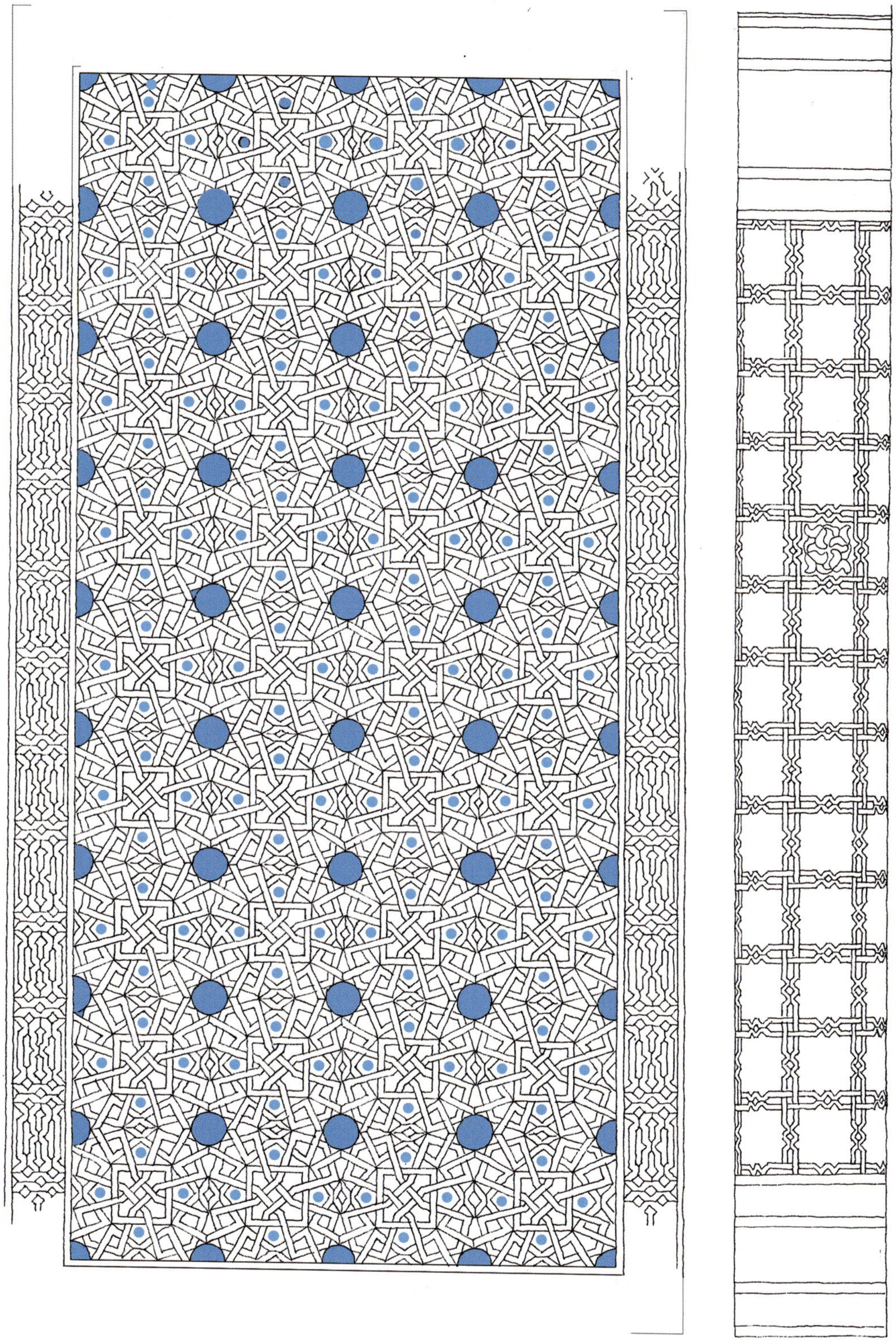

Figure 3.10: Reconstruction drawing of one of the side-panels of the portal niche, scale: 1:20.

Figure 3.9 (opposite page): The Ghurid side panel preserved on the right side of the portal niche.

Figure 3.11: Detail picture of side panel made of terracotta elements.

Each side panel were framed by a 19 cm wide band of shaped bricks, around the full design of the panel measuring two metres wide and four metres high. Perhaps influenced by art of the carpet weaving patterns of the time, the panels were divided in a grid making 9 x 4 squares of 40 cm x 40 cm, the corners of which were marked by 10 cm (in diameter) turquoise-blue glazed ceramic domes (actually externally glazed bottoms of pottery). Each glazed dome made centre of chain-like interlinked geometric designs expanded into an interwoven pattern made of terracotta elements, making combinations of octagons, trapezoids and squares established within more complicated polygons (probably related

Figure 3.12: We temporarily recreated the effect of painted sides of the terracotta elements using perishable water colours. (See also text page 94 below figure 6.8).

to "the golden section"). The spaces created inbetween, as pentagons, were also filled in by smaller turquoise blue glazed circular pins. (See chapter seven, figure 7.9-7.10 for a schematic drawing of generic geometry of these panels).

THE GHURID VAULT

The vault roofing and the niche of the 12th century Ghurid portal is an interesting architectural and structural detail. First the sides of the rectangular bay is linked with two arches, each aligned with the

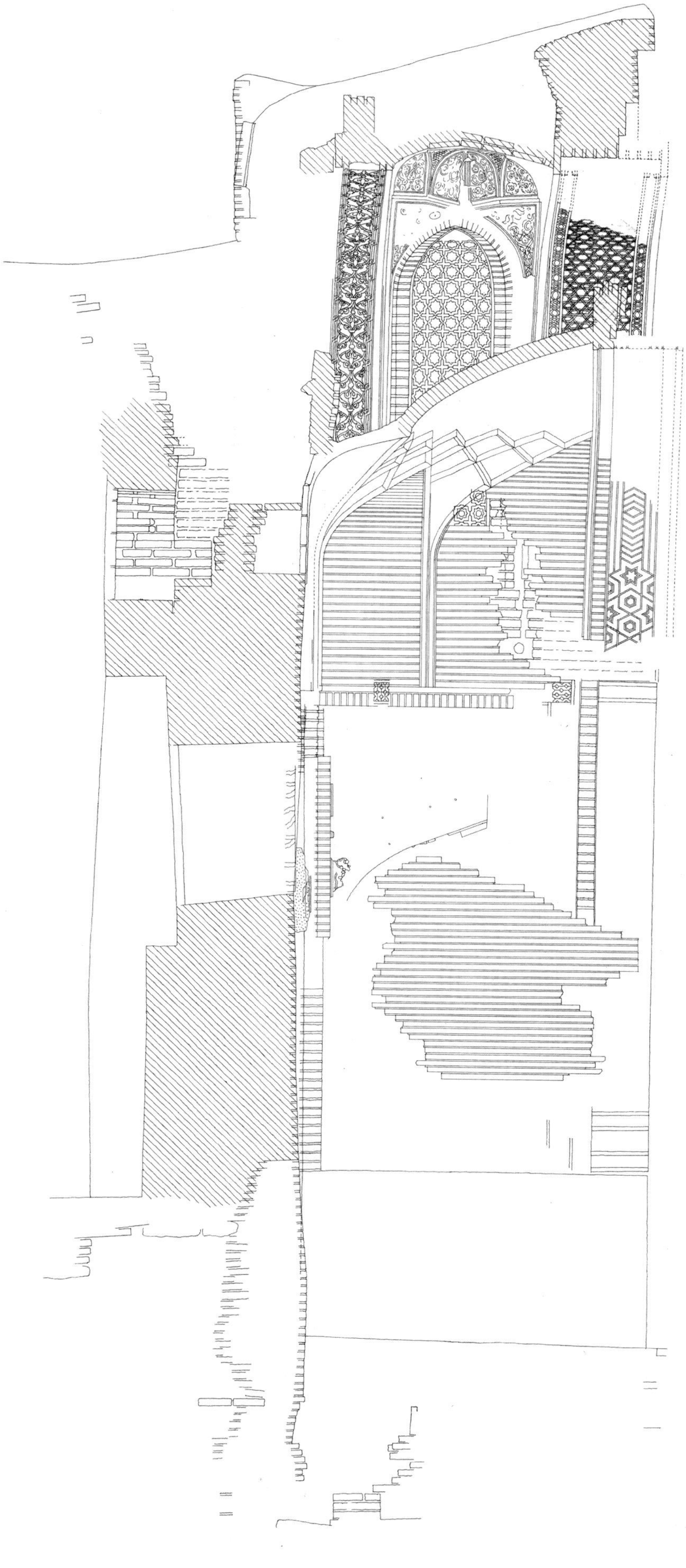

Ghurid arch and top of the vault with stucco decorations of 12th century.

The Timurid arch of 15th century.

Timurid vault with star shape ceiling and rib decoration and fine masonry.

The Timurid surface glazed tile-work covering the Ghurid terracotta work.

The Timurid decorative masonry also covering the Ghurid columns.

Figure 3.13: Measured drawing of the section of the Ghurid portal, where the Timurid vault and works are also visible. Scale: 1:50. Erik Hansen, 1964.

Figure 3.14: Structure and decoration of the Ghurid vault in the portal. It shows both terracotta elements of decoration sat in soffit of the inner arches of the portal as well as decoration carved in gypsum plasters at corners and ceiling of the vault.

surface lines of the structure; the main arch at the front of the structure is about 100 cm deep and the arch at the back about 47 cm. The distance between the arches is 1.43 m.

The two side-walls, continuing up to the vault, are built with curved decorative niches having 23 cm recession at their central depth. These niches create both decorative parts but also structural formation; at the height of 9.75 m from the ground level, these arches reduce the span from 4.48 m to 3.64 m (figure 4.6 Plan IV). Brick projections higher up reduce the span of the niche to 3.30 m, which makes

Figure 3.15: Soffit of the structural Ghurid front arch.

the base of the vaulting and the ceiling. By applying further decorative divisions, like muqarnases, the vaulted ceiling is formed.

The soffits of the main and structural Ghurid arches are decorated with a series of terracotta elements laid in a plaster bed, establishing an array of modular repetition and interwoven geometric patterns (figures 3.15, 7.11 and 7.12)

The vault and its base arches are decorated in plaster with floral carvings (figures 3.13, 3.14, 3.16, 7.13 and 7.14). ▪

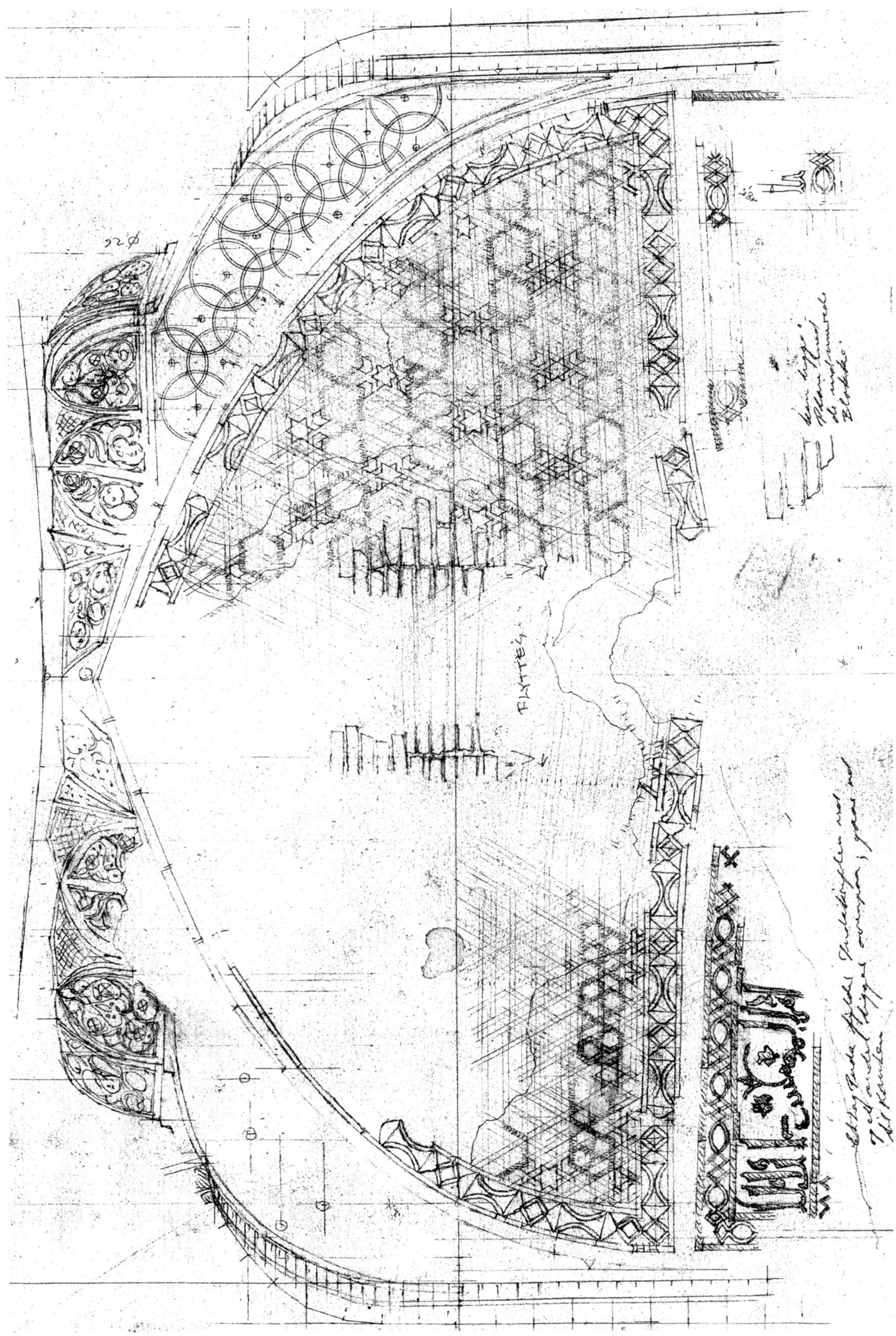

Figure 3.16: The Ghurid upper niche and the vault section, Measured drawing by E. Hansen 1964, reproduced in scale 1:20.

Figure 4.1: The portal of the Ghurids seen from the south-east before its restoration in 1964. In the floor is an opening to the water channel draining the ablution pool inside the courtyard of the mosque.

CHAPTER 4

THE REBUILDING BY THE TIMURIDS

When damages and decay in the building of the Friday Mosque advanced in the 15th century it became necessary for the Timurid rulers of Herat to repair and restore this prestigious historic building. Under supervision of minister Ali-Sher Nawayee, the Timurids maintained and repaired the structure of the Ghurid Portal.

The roof and ceiling decoration of the Ghurid arch of the portal had been damaged considerably and the top of the Ghurid inscription probably did not exist.

Conservation of the remaining Ghurid parts of the portal was possible, instead of destroying the old roofing. The solution the Timurids adopted was the construction of a new roofing below the old one, followed by redecoration of the flat parts of the portal; this procedure of resurfacing could not have been easily applied at the curved surface of the Ghurid vault and ceiling. It was a question of first filling up all the uneven surfaces of the Ghurid inscription and level them with a meagre mortar, then to install new tile panels.

Fortunately (from our point of view) this renewal would not result in a destruction of the existing building or its parts, but by adding a newer layer of art work they were covering it with a new surface on top of the old one and introduced style and proportions that was state of the art of the Timurid time and somehow different to the proportions used by the Ghurids. Accordingly, they would preserve most of the portal. They only had to remove wall decorations inside the bay where the new roofing had to be supported (figures 3.4 and 3.5).

THE TIMURID DECORATION ON THE GHURID PORTAL

The new covering consisted of prefabricated sheets and thin panels in the then well practiced tiling technique, *koshi-kari*, which consisted of inlay of fragments of cut-tile making a multi-coloured glazed mosaic of geometric or vegetal composition and forms. The panels were assembled as 5-8 cm thick plates of convenient size for installation, a technique which will be described in detail in chapter eight.

In 1964 very little of the frontal facade of the Ghurid Portal was covered by Timurid decoration as the monument had been left in neglect of maintenance for long. Traces of the monumental Ghurid inscription were visible under the plaster layer (figures 4.2, 6.2, 6.3 and 8.6). It was different for the inner facades of the structure where the Timurids work had remained untouched also during the later works of the 20th century renewals, and surely the important parts could still be preserved. The panel on the inside left wall (southern side of niche) exhibits well the material and technique of the Timurids (figures 4.3 and 4.4). It is showing a surface brick work making imitation of a blank arcade above which is a tile decoration richly designed in floral patterns of yellow, blue and white glazing. Underneath where the plaster has fallen off, we distinguish parts of the Ghurid work (figure 4.4).

Figure 4.2: The Ghurid Portal before restoration.

Above the floral design, decoration of surface work was made of yet another Timurid style: a design made of mixing unglazed elements with glazed tiles (figure 8.5). The vertical part of the vault was made as imitation of the surface of masonry with black joints executed precisely in white faience plates with black joints.

THE NEW ARCH AND VAULT OF THE TIMURIDS

The Timurid builder's wanted to make a new ceiling, an entrance iwan in the form of a half dome vault placed between the massive projection walls of the Ghurid portal. They built their main arch a meter and half below the old arch that supported the Ghurid structure, which could be preserved as it was.

Figure 4.3: The southern side of the Timurid arch and vault before restoration.

Figure 4.5: The damaged status of the Timurid vault before restoration. At the bottom is seen remains of the lower part of the vault construction with crossing ribs. The Timurid work was so thin that when damaged the Ghurid works behind becomes visible.

Figure 4.4 (opposite page): On the left side (south side) of the portal niche starting from the substructure, part of the Timurid wall decoration was well preserved, extending to the Timurid vault above. This could be preserved in situ during the restoration in 1964.

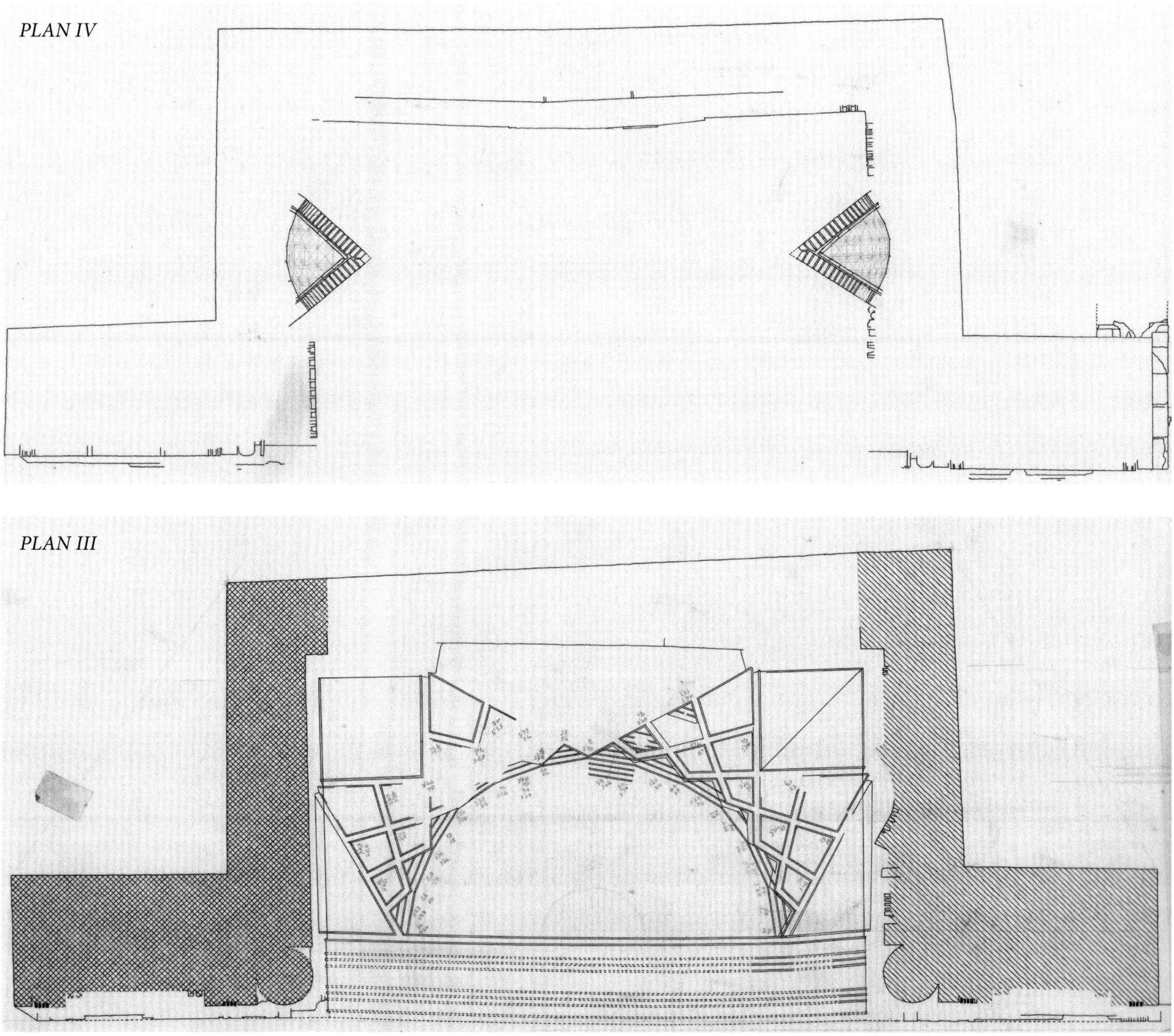

Figure 4.6: Measured drawings of the plans at different height levels of the structure of the Ghurid portal showing the Timurid half-vault (plan III) and above it at the base of the Ghurid vault (plan IV). Scale: 1:50. Erik Hansen, 1964.

Note that the details recorded in these plans indicate different levels relatively i.e. the left side details shows plan under the section-line while the details at the right indicate the plan above the same section line.

Figure 4.7: The Timurid ceiling at the Ghurid portal after restoration.

This would also have the advantage that the new vault should only carry itself and therefore could be a lighter construction.

The Timurid vault was built up with a detailing known as the *karbandi* technique: construction of crossing arches in order to narrow up the span for the base of a dome of an iwan.

The work probably began with the construction of the front arch. This work needed solid scaffolding.

Afterwards the 12 structural ribs would be made, either prefabricated or made in place of bricks and gypsum mortar, supported by light scaffolding. Their first part is made like a corner arch to prepare the rectangular bay for an octagonal like transition zone and then to work up the required sub-arches (near the wall) all like pointed arches crossing the other (figures 4.3, 4.5, 4.6 plan III and 4.7).

Then, the spaces between the ribs structure would be filled in by bricks laid in mortar aligned with the curves of the design.

Finally the shell construction could continue from the zigzag frame making its star shaped base towards the centre of the half-dome, guided by segments of arches extended upwards and pointing to

Figure 4.8: The transition from the *karbandi* section to the circular section of the dome.

the centre of the half-dome. We suppose that this work was directed from the underside of the dome. But the last hole in the middle with a diameter of 50 cm should be closed by a wedge in the form of a ready-made block (figure 4.9). Strengthened with an additional plaster layer applied from the top, the whole would look and function as one halfcircular base of the dome structure.

Koshi medallions are inserted in the polygons in the *karbandi* section and continued to the skirt of the half dome. This part of the construction is covered by floral designs of glazed *Koshi* elements in white, blue and yellow guided by black concentric circles, and decreasing in size towards the centre of the dome. We remark the geometrically precise execution of this work. The brick work also holds tile

Figure 4.9: The upper part of the relatively well preserved Timurid ceiling seen from beneath. The central part, moon like ceiling covered by small *koshi* fragments was probably inserted from the top.

panels and finish up with the moon formed central area (figure 4.9). The tile decorations are produced in rich multi-coloured floral decorations, perhaps symbolizing the blue sky full of stars in the region's bright nights. Figure 8.3 shows a total view of this remarkable dome structure. ▪

Figure 5.1: Kabul Museum, where the Afghan technicians clean the panels from Lashkari Bazaar (Helmand) for installation as permanent exhibition on the wall inside Kabul Museum, Darul-Aman, Kabul.

CHAPTER 5

RESTORATION IN AFGHANISTAN 1964

THE CONFERENCE IN VENICE

The year 1964 was declared by UNESCO as "the year of the historical monuments", and a great international conference on this subject was held in Venice in May of that year. A rather important contribution from the side of Afghanistan was the impressive presentation by Dr. Ahmad Ali Motamedi, the director of Kabul museum, that caused admiration and remark for how much the conservation of the cultural heritage would mean for the self-consideration of a small and poor country in development.

Restoration and conservation were not unknown problems for the architects of the 19th century, and very often the aim of a restoration could have been to bring a monument back to its "original state", even if there was no exact trace of such a state, and in that way through the restoration process many important parts from later periods of the structure could disappear. The French architect Violet le Duc (l. 1814-1879) was specially known for his restorations in that way. In another way, particularly in England, through the architect James Ruskin (l. 1819-1900) it was claimed that even the ruin had its beauty and had the right to "die in peace". Then, in the 20th century the attraction of "modernism" turned people's interests away from the history, looking towards the future. After World War II other directions of thinking were realized. Colonial thinking turned interests towards the more anonymous architecture, and through UNESCO an understanding of foreign cultures was increased.

The aim of the conference in Venice was to discuss and create guide-lines for that new situation. They were published by the end of the conference as the "Charter of Venice", which is still a valuable reference, although many conditions have changed. The main point here was, as far as possible, that any feature of a building is part of its history and should be respected.

Dr. Motamedi gave a lecture on two recent restorations of historic buildings in Afghanistan. The first was the Buddhist monastery of Guldara in the region of Kabul sponsored by UNESCO under direction of the French architect Alexandre Lézine. The second was an Islamic Mausoleum of Sultan Abdur Razaq in Ghazni, sponsored by the Italian embassy in Kabul, under the direction of the Italian architect Andrea Bruno in 1961.

The Buddhist stupa was made of the local shale stone gathered in the neighbourhood of the monastery. These stones were carefully reused and placed in horizontal courses as dry masonry without mortar. The mausoleum in Ghazni was made of burned bricks assembled with lime mortar. In both cases, for their restoration, the essential question to consider was whether to repair, stabilize or to renew the broken parts of the construction's masonry; eventually to complete certain parts, where it could be desirable for the consolidation or presentation of the monument. For execution of the work, however, the architects' intentions in the two aforementioned cases were quite different. While A. Lézine aimed, in the case of the stupa, to reproduce the original material and technique as nearly as possible

Figure 5.2 (a, b): Two examples of conservation works in Afghanistan in 1961-62: A. Lezine's work at the Buddhist stupa of Guldara in Logar (left) and the conservation work by A. Bruno at the Mausoleum of Abdul Razaq in Ghazni (right).

A. Bruno in restoration of the mausoleum intended to follow the new ideals introduced by the Italian conservators, namely that later repairs and introduction of new elements should be clearly visible. Therefore, for new masonry Bruno used new bricks, and the line of the new surfaces finishing into the historic was clearly marked by colour jointing. Such different professional customs were occasion to adverse critics in Kabul, which finished at the level of the ambassadors, and the Afghans asked; "Which method is the right one, the French or the Italian?"

This question, in fact, was regarded as one of the main problems discussed by the participants in the Venice conference, and was to clarify guide-lines for future works of restoration: "The Venice Charter" for the Conservation and Restoration of Monuments and Sites, 31 May 1964 is a code of professional standards that gives an international framework for the preservation and restoration of ancient buildings. It is important to notice, that Erik Hansen did not receive information of the charter before he returned to Denmark from Afghanistan.

THE FIRST AFGHAN RESTORATION PROJECT

Kabul museum, after the discussion on the aforementioned two cases of restorations, as the next step decided to establish its own restoration department in 1964. In this case the Danish architect Erik Hansen was the adviser and five young technicians from the Vocational School of Kabul, a German established school of crafts (*Maktab-i-Sanae*), were associated. They were Sultan Fayaz, Babamurad Feragi, Said Azim Reha, Mohammad Sharif and Qayum, together with an administrative representative from the office, Sadeq. As an exercise the team began working with the installation in the Museum

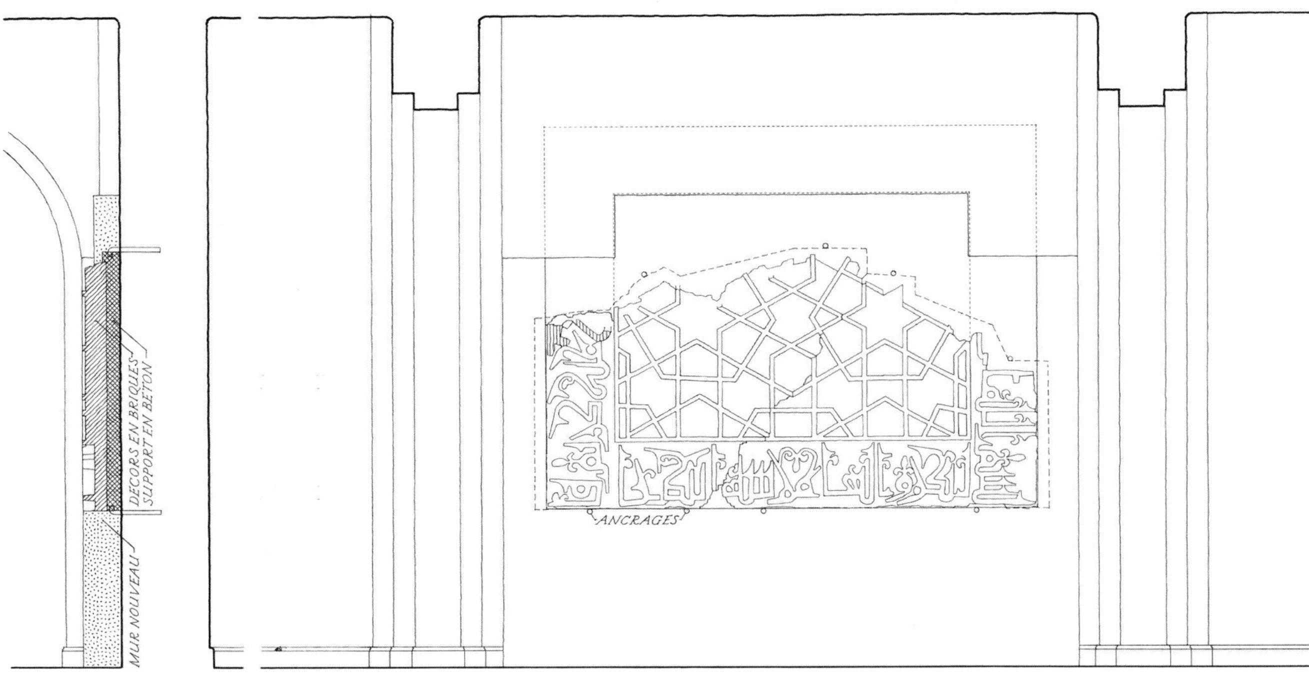

Figure 5.3: Measured drawing of the Lashkari Bazaar wall decorations installed in Kabul Museum in 1964. The inscription is Koran sura 27, verses 40 and 41. Scale 1:50. Erik Hansen, 1964.

building of two objects from the French excavations in the Ghaznavid palace of Lashkari Bazaar, Helmand.

The first object was a part of a large wall decoration from the audience hall of the Masud palace and executed as a panel of tiles and bricks. For the purpose of its transport the archaeologists had attached a cement plate. The other object was a small Mihrab of clay attached to a wooden skeletal. Both were excellent objects for exhibition in the museum, and in the case of the mihrab it had the exact dimensions for being placed in one of the smaller rooms of the museum building. The later had many broken parts where the plaster needed to be repaired and completed. But the young technicians soon got very engaged in this new exercise and Sharif contributed with the bright idea to colour the new parts with dust kicked up from the soil. But a small incident arrived; in the period when the team was going to install the Mihrab Dr. Motamedi was absent. His assistant would stop the work objecting that the Mihrab did not place towards the direction of Mecca, as it ought to be in real circumstances, and it did not matter that here it actually was not a real mosque but a museum object. Finally it was accepted when we promised to place a label to tell why it had not been possible to place the Mihrab in the right direction. Another visitor who heard that Erik Hansen was not a Muslim praised him for having come so far away for restoration of their mosque.

The Afghan team got the hands-on experience and impression of the existence of the monumental heritage in their country and perception on the importance to conserving them.

Figure 5.4 (a, b): Decorative wall panel from Lashkari bazaar (Helmand) installed on the walls of the Kabul museum asa permanent exhibition, 1964

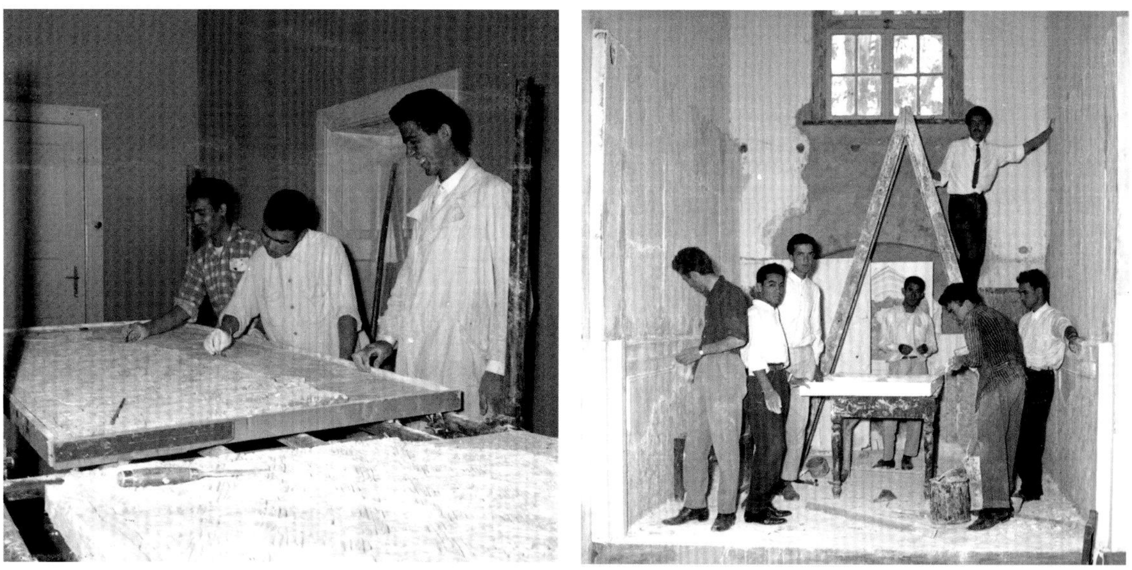

Figure 5.5 (a, b): Installation of the Masud mosque from palace of Lashkari bazaar (Helmand) in Kabul museum as a permanent exhibition, 1964.

THE MONUMENTS AND CONSERVATION WEEK

The main purpose of Erik Hansen's stay for one year in Afghanistan was the restoration of the portal of the Ghurids in Herat. However, he also participated in an awareness project, as he reported to UNESCO in 1965.

"Another assignment with this mission was that we (me and my wife Inger Kickan Hansen) together should prepare illustrations by survey and photography of the general status of the most important

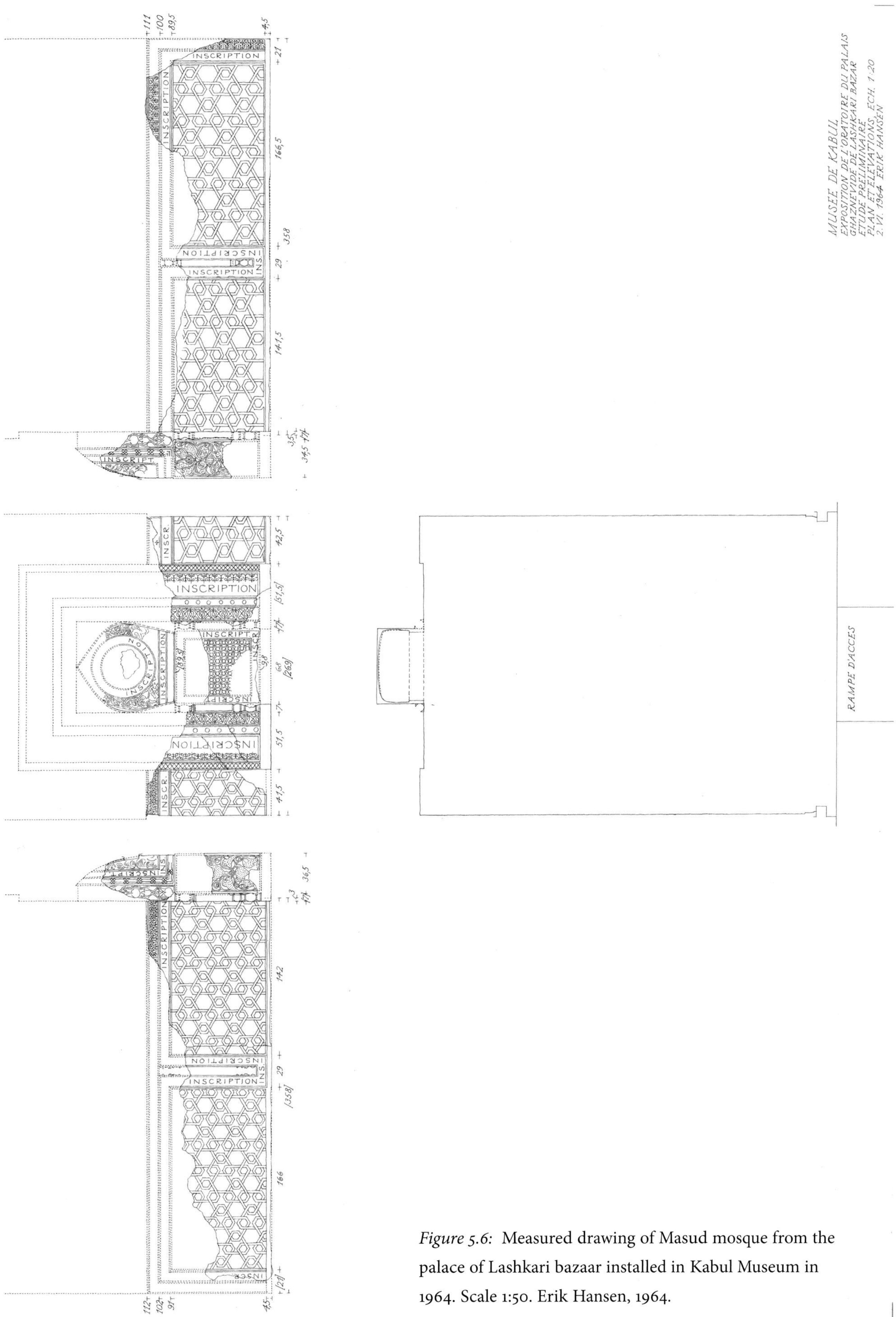

Figure 5.6: Measured drawing of Masud mosque from the palace of Lashkari bazaar installed in Kabul Museum in 1964. Scale 1:50. Erik Hansen, 1964.

Figure 5.7: The Masud mosque from Lashkari Bazaar installed in Kabul Museum. The chamber survived the civil war during which the museum building was looted and burned. Photo: C. Christensen, 2012.

historic monuments of Afghanistan, their state of conservation and need for protection. This task was with a double intention: Survey and documentation, and photographs to be used for an exhibition in Kabul in relation with the "Week of historic monuments" in August that year. This survey which was performed country wide included several sections:

1. The Islamic monuments of Ghazni
2. The Buddhist monuments around Kabul
3. The Buddhist statues of Bamiyan
4. The monuments of Lashkari bazaar (Helmand)
5. The monuments of Herat
6. Finally the region of the north of Afghanistan – Mazar-i-Sharif and Balkh.

The "week of the historic monuments" was in relation to the conference of Venice of May 1964 that was celebrated in several European cities with the purpose to attract the attention of the historic architecture and its importance as a part of our culture. So in the case of Afghanistan, such celebration began with a speech of Dr. Motamedi opening the exhibition of 62 photographs in size 50x60 cm, and a drawing contest by the school children in Kabul. In addition to the rich collection of Buddhist and Islamic art in the museum one could also see the two installations of the historic panels from Lashkari bazaar implemented by the five young technicians / restorers of the museum.

Figure 5.8 (a, b, c & d): Pictures of the ceremony (speeches by Dr. Motamedi and Erik Hansen) and giving awards by Dr Motamedi to school children who participated in a drawing contest, and exhibition in occasion of the Monuments Week of Afghanistan, 1964.

Ceremony of the last evening of the "Week of the historic monuments" included placing torches on the old fortification on the *Sherdarwaza* mountain walls, arranged by the boy-scouts, which illuminated the top of the mountain walls.

Few days later the five young restorers parted for Herat with the scaffoldings from the museum and to begin the restoration of the Ghurid portal of the Friday Mosque of Herat." ▪

Erik Hansen, 1965

CHAPTER 6

RESTORATION OF THE GHURID PORTAL 1964

The following text is based upon a translation of an extract from a report (in Danish), which Erik Hansen wrote to friends and colleges during and immediately after his work in Herat.

Around the year 1200, while the Danes were building the extraordinary five tower church in Kalundborg in Denmark, the Ghurids started building the Friday Mosque in Herat: A large open praying yard surrounded by four huge iwans opening to the courtyard. Along the circumference of the building and behind the iwans ran an arched corridor, which was used for processions during the festival, and a magnificent portal which led to a forest of columns carrying dimly lit arches.

The Ghurids had their capital Firuzkuh in Ghur, situated in the central highland 2000 meter above sea level. They made real the dream of all central Asian small kingdoms: To control the countries south and north of the Hindu-Kush mountain range and to conquer India. Their strength was the impassable mountain tracks in their own country. Their weakness was that they had to return from the summer battles before the snow blocked their way home.

To review briefly the background, explained in chapter one and two, their power was annihilated by the Mongol invasion under Genghis Khan in the beginning of the 13th century and maybe the work on the Friday Mosque in Herat was never completed and additions were made by rulers coming afterwards. In 1409-1447, Shah Rukh, the fourth son of Timurlane was the ruler of Herat, and together with his gifted wife Gawhadshad they developed the city and its architecture. The greatest artists and scientists of the time gathered in Herat, and the renaissance of Asia emerged. The Timurids also restored and decorated the Friday Mosque.

After centuries of decay a new extensive restoration started in our time: Most of old decoration in tile mosaic was removed and new tiles were mounted instead. Iranian craftsmen made a new school of decoration. Now the restoration was coming to its end the school had existed nearly 40 years. If one follows the different sections of the decorations one will find a development towards richer, more flourishing and technically better styles. An old architectural monument has been destroyed, but a new one has been created. However, the huge main portal was untouched by the contemporary restoration.

In agreement with the Afghan authorities the Kabul museum selected the portal for restoration (1964), because it posed particularly interesting conservation problems.

Figure 6.1 (Opposite page): The conservation team who worked on the restoration of the Ghurid portal in Herat in 1964. From left to right: Architect Erik Hansen, Sultan Fayaz. M. Sharif, Said Azim Reha, Qayum, and Baba Murad Faraghi (sitting) – on the roof top of the Friday Mosque of Herat, 1964.

Figure 6.2: The upper-right part of the facade of the Ghurid portal before restoration in 1964.

When the Timurids had covered the entire facade of the Ghurid arch they had lowered the arch of the gate entrance. Above the arch the Timurid facade had fallen down so one could see the Ghurid arch with its decoration in stucco (figs. 4.1-4.2). But the general impression of the monument was an entangled maze of mortar, the base for the fallen Timurid decoration.

A more typical restoration task could have hardly been found: Should one show the Ghurid monument one had to remove the Timurid additions, or would one present the Timurid monument one had to hide the decorative Ghurid façade and the inscription which nobody (after Timurids) had read. Earlier, architect Lézine had proposed to remove the Timurid arch and façade decorations and to restore the Ghurid monument. This was the French method [Violet le Duc method]. But we were thinking on the Danish Roman village churches with original fresco painting which had been cut across

Figure 6.3 (a, b): The process of removal of the fragments of the Timurid tiled layer

by Gothic arches. Nowadays Danes would hesitate very much to remove the Gothic arches to show the Roman paintings. We were also remembering the gentle restoration of frescoes made by conservator Lind who only cleaned and preserved. He did not complete the fresco paintings.

We reflected: "We for sure recognized the Ghurid architecture as the greatest, but our grandparents would probably have preferred the floral style of the Timurids to the bold geometrical decoration of the Ghurids."

A large number of magnificent Timurid monuments exist in Herat, Samarkand and Mashhad while Ghurid architecture is known only from a few monuments, but the fact that the Timurids had another taste and meant to do better was history and justified preservation.

As the first impression during the documentation of the portal, we considered just to remove the visible mortar and leave the Timurid arch and the few remaining pieces of their façade decorations. From an archaeological viewpoint this would give full information of the Ghurid monument and permit reading of the inscription. But it would have been a very technical restoration and it would have not allowed the viewer to conceive the monument as a complete work of art.

A scaffold was raised for studying the building more closely and we began recording measurements for documentation. It was a terrible scaffold made of crooked wooden branches joined with iron cramps and wires (as figure 8.15). It was hair-raising to see the workers balancing bare-footed on the slippery round timber carrying huge loads. On the top they made a floor of thin boards from crates and with great fear we climbed the terrifying construction the strength of which had no correlation to the amounts of wood used for it.

The Timurid arch was studied in detail and we found that it was constructed out of thin ribs and fillings consisting of the tile mosaic itself, with its 3-4 cm thick back-layer of plaster. The arch was covered by a thin layer of brick tiles. This gave us the idea to dismantle the Timurid arch with decoration and rebuild it in another place. In this way we would have two monuments instead of one. The officials

Figure 6.4: The two arches: The remains of the 12th century Ghurid work and 15th century conservation by the Timurids, before start of the restoration work of 1964.

with whom we had been in contact had expressed their desire to build a new museum in Herat, and the Timurid portal could find a suitable place as entrance.

With these thoughts in mind we left Herat and drove through the central highland passing the madrassa (Koran school) in Chesht (figures 1.6 and 7.4) and the minaret in Jam (Firuzkoh) (figures 1.1, 1.7 and 7.5), the only other significant monuments we knew from the Ghurids. The two large cupolas in Chesht were photographed for the first time by the German war expedition Niedermeyer in 1917. The minaret in Jam was discovered in 1957 and the portal in Herat would so to say come back into light now.

Figure 6.5: The terracotta prefabricated elements used in decorative work (wall and the soffit of inner arch) at the upper inside part of the Ghurid portal. The crescent shaped area has floral patterns carved in gypsum.

We returned in the beginning of October to start the restoration. Five of the Kabul museum craftsmen who should be educated as building restorers had arrived a few days earlier with materials, tools and the pipe scaffold belonging to the museum. They nearly had finished erecting the pipe scaffold.

Our good friend fresco conservator Erik Olsson from Gotland in Sweden had come to visit us and he had followed us to Herat to work together with us. He used his holidays for it but – as he said – it happens only once that you are given the possibility to restore a Ghurid monument. We were very grateful to be able to use his experience, especially when we dismantled the Timurid tile decorations. It turned out that ordinary carpenter's glue was suitable to glue canvas on the surface (figure 6.3).

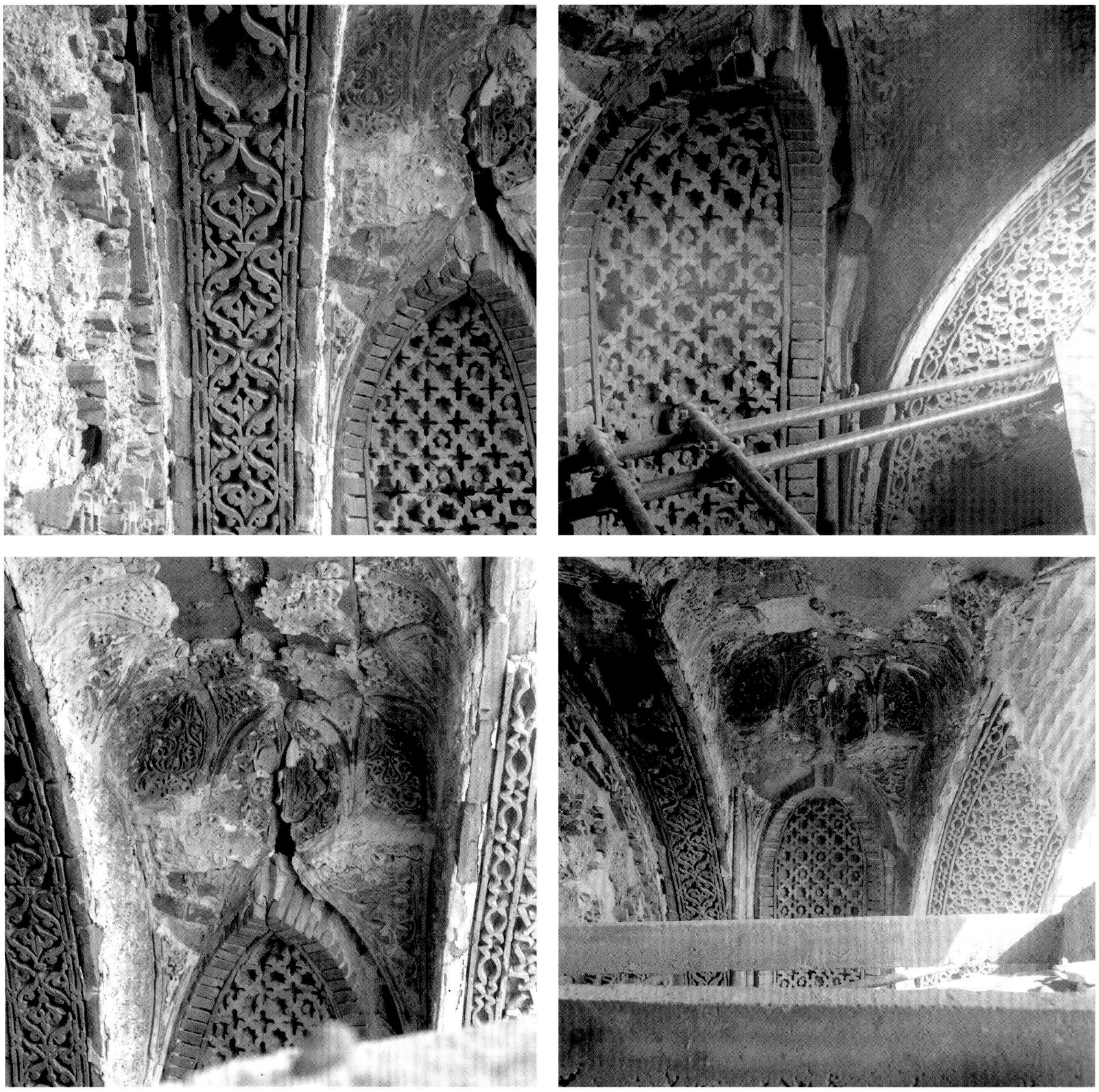

Figure 6.6 (a, b, c, d): The ceiling of the Ghurid vault was made of squinches and fine arches sitting on the two main arches of the structure. The vault had a severe crack. Figure d shows the vault after restoration with the two concrete beams which support the arch of the Timurid vault.

Afterwards the decoration could be loosened from the back with long iron bars. Finally the glue and canvas could be removed with hot water after casting a thin layer of reinforced concrete on the back of the plate.

As soon as we had erected the scaffold to a sufficient height we made an extension between the two arches in order to inspect the Ghurid arch more in detail. It then turned out that it was less well preserved than we had expected. One wall was cracked apart, the arch had sunk and a large part of the stucco ornamentation on the arch had disappeared and the decoration on the rear wall was seriously damaged (figures 6.4-6.7).

Fig. 6.7 (a, b, c, d): Ghurid decoration on the northern side wall partially covered by Timurid decorative masonry. The lower part of the masonry was removed. The crack in the upper part was repaired.

It then became obvious that we would only loose by removing the well preserved Timurid arch. Luckily one side of the archway had the Timurid tile surface well preserved (figures 4.3 and 4.4) while it had nearly disappeared from the opposite side (figures 4.1 and 6.7c), meaning that the Ghurid decoration on that side could be completely restored and made visible without destroying a lot of Timurid tiles. On the front of the building the relatively small remaining areas with Timurid tiles could be removed and preserved (figures 6.2 and 6.3) so the Ghurid decoration could be restored as a whole.

Figure 6.8 (a, b): Left side of the Portal wall where one can see the start of the Kufic glazed inscription and the decorative round corner column. Figure (a) before and figure (b) after restauration.

In this manner it was possible to let both of the monuments be restored at the same time with very few changes. Each of the monuments would not disturb the other and the history of the building would still be visible. This meant that our task was limited to cleaning and consolidation.

Little by little the Ghurid decoration appeared from behind the thick layers of mortar, which we removed and we discovered a very refined technique: The geometrical decoration itself, on the vertical inside of the niche, was made of tiny shaped bricks the sides of which had been painted, some with cinnabar red other with verdigris green according to a specific system. If one look at the decoration from the front it has the yellow colour of the raw brick with dark spaces in between, but if one look sideways the colour plays in red and green, a kind of "movement in the art". We had to drop our former admiration for the Ghurids restrained selection of materials and accept their "barbaric" joy for the colours which made this architecture stranger but also much more captivating than we could have imagined.

The cleaning work was difficult. The Timurid mortar was often very hard and sat on a fragile base but we got the experience little by little. Loose parts of the decoration were glued on immediately, sometimes reinforced by thick copper wire which we obtained from the power station.

Many people came to look at the work maybe first of all to admire our pipe scaffold, but one morning, as I stood drawing, five afghan wise men in long kaftans with white turbans on their heads arrived. They remained standing in the yard eagerly discussing. The leader in the discussion was a small shrunken person with a high pitched voice. Presently he was climbing the scaffold and while ascending from level to level he was yelling eagerly to the others below. Then I understood that he was able to read kufic writing and that he was the first in our time who received a message written 750 years earlier. He promised to return when more of the text had appeared so he could read all of it.

After some weeks we had to go to Kabul and returned one month later. We were met by a wonderful sight: The complete front was cleaned and it was obvious that it is an unusual monument with fine proportions. It was one of the finest in the country, on the same level as the minaret in Jam.

Figure 6.9: The Ghurid portal during the restoration work; the inscription had been cleaned of the fragments of the plaster and deteriorated Timurid remains.

The large blue Kufic inscription stood well preserved starting on the lower right corner and ending on the lower left corner, only missing on the top of the arch. Translation of the Arabic text read: *The glorious Sultan, the divine king of the kings, lord of the peoples, ruler of the Arabs and the non-Arabs ... his kingdom, may his highness be unattainable, his achievement splendid and his throne stand above all. Ramadan 597.* (also see figure 3.1 and 3.6). This was the eulogy connected to the name of the famous Ghurid sultan Ghyath-ul-din, the same as on the minaret in Jam. So it was him who in the year 1200 (year 597 according to the Muslim calendar) had built the large Friday Mosque in Herat.

Now the difficult consolidation works remained. After the mortar had been removed we could see that the foundation was heavily undermined partly because of weathering from a drain channel (figure 4.1) partly because a kiln for tiles formerly had been built alongside the building. One side of

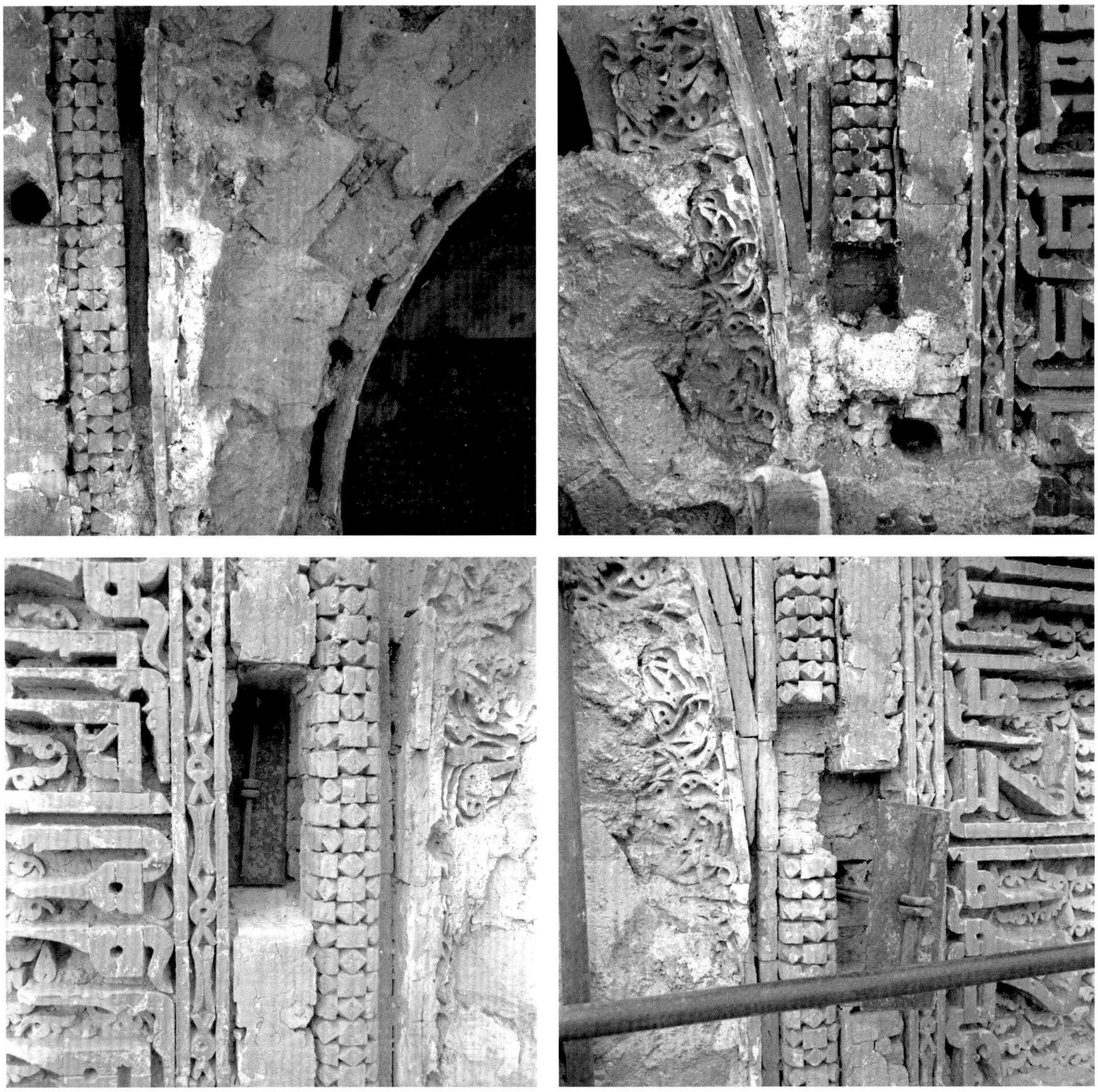

Figure 6.10 (a, b, c, d): Holes from the deteriorated wood tie rods (a, b). New steel tie rods inserted during restoration (c, d).

the façade had cracked loose and was leaning heavily outwards and the arches from the mosque behind were pressing the rear wall forward.

It had been clear from the beginning that most of the cracks in the portal originated from the pressure by the arched column hall behind and from the meter-thick layer of clay which covered the roof of the mosque. Furthermore it looked like the water was seeping down between the clay and the rear wall of the portal where it could freeze during winter and press even more on the rear wall. Historically the structure was reinforced with wooden poles seen on both sides of the Arch (figure 6.10 a-b) but the wood had deteriorated.

So we started to dig down into the roof behind the portal to reach the surface of the roof arches.

Figure 6.11 (a, b, c, d): Removal of roof above Ghurid vault and digging down to make space for reinforced concrete beam.

During this work we found that the rear wall of the monument was built of burned bricks using clay as mortar. This meant that we had to re-build that part if it was to last. Finally we would need to fit a strong reinforced concrete beam which could transfer the lateral load from the roof arches around the portal.

But no matter how far we dug down we did not seem to reach the arches. Little by little the clay was substituted by a packing of clay bricks. When we disassembled the rear wall it turned out that it was as continuation of the same packing of clay bricks. We no longer knew where the clay stopped and the wall started and we feared that we could dismantle the complete monument without reaching anything solid. We realized that the Ghurid builders had been artists, not building technicians with thoughts of building something to last.

Figure 6.12 (a, b, c, d): Removal of rear wall (a, b, c) of Ghurid vault and digging down to make space for reinforced concrete beam. The steel tie rod for the right hand side of the portal can be seen (d).

We now had so much clay and bricks spread over the roof of the mosque so we feared that the extra load might cause cracks in the roof arches below. Our dug-out was so deep that we had to support the sides as safety precaution.

At the same time the workers had removed the recent repairs of the foundation. It was made of brick fragments set in clay mortar. Even here we had to dig deep to reach the hard undamaged foundation. It turned out that this foundation was made of hard burned bricks set in a mixture of lime and ashes. This mortar was very strong and resilient. It is a mortar which is still used in Herat for making water proof tile work in bathrooms. We had supported the front of the monument the best way we could with our scaffold pipes, not that we were sure that they could do anything else other than delay the

Figure 6.13 (a, b): Lower part of the walls of the Ghurid portal, below the inscription level was quite damaged and had to be repaired (a). The original corners of wall became visible when the later-built wall blocking the portal was cut for archaeological inspection of the masonry lines at the foundation level (b).

collapsing of the wall so the workers could escape. We used mortar with cement for the additional foundations and managed to do the work without accidents.

We had finally reached the roof arches and solid wall of the monument. The arches in the front of the Ghurid vault and of the Timurid vault were constructed of gypsum plaster according to the common method used in the region. But after the degradation of the surface and penetration of water this plaster had lost its strength and the arches were partially crumbling. The weak sections were dismantled and redone: the arches with a core of reinforced concrete connected with the rear wall by steel anchors for the Ghurid arch and by two beams of reinforced concrete for the Timurid arch (figure 6.6 d). A large beam of reinforced concrete was integrated into the construction to receive the pressure from the arches from the mosque halls in the back.

The wooden forms and the iron reinforcement were in place and we were ready to make the casting. We were fighting against the calendar because it was the middle of December and the weather was getting cold. The concrete mixing had to be made with pre-heated water and all the concrete had to be carried to the roof by the workers. They did a marvellous job only encouraged by some extra lunch and double payment. At 6 PM the work was finished and covered by straw. The building was saved from collapse.

The rear wall was reconstructed afterwards from the old bricks and using bastard mortar (figure 6.14). All the reinforcements made of modern materials are invisible. For all visible sections we have re-used old bricks. The penetration of water was stopped by providing a proper roof drainage canal behind the monument.

The Ghurid vault, a very fragile construction covered by a coat of soil, was reinforced and the top was covered by a slab of reinforced concrete, asphalt and mud straw plaster "*kah-gel*".

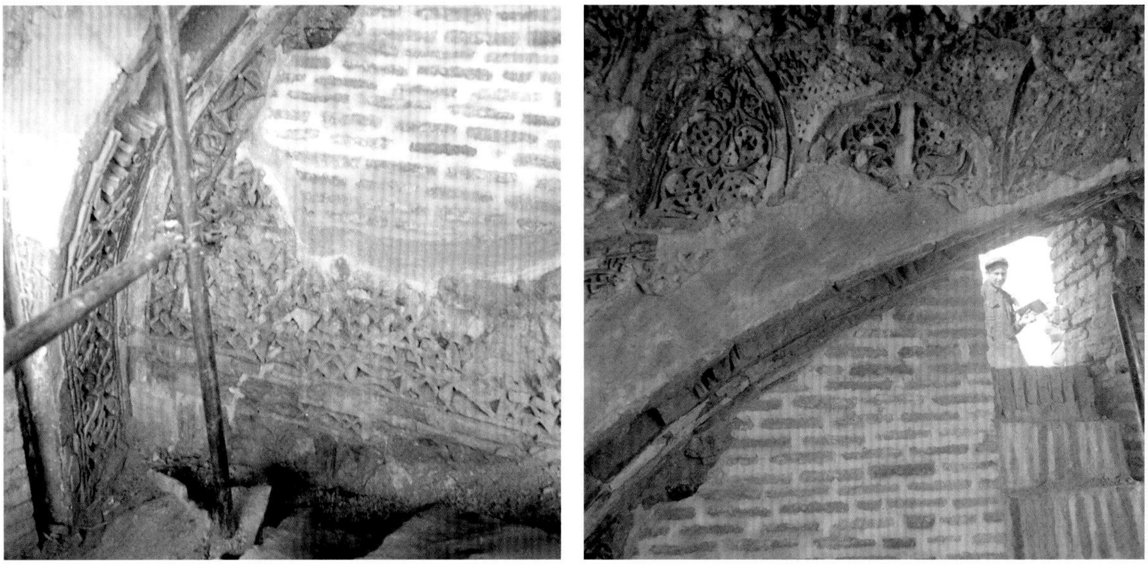

Figure 6.14 (a, b, c): The Ghurid vault and back wall after the restoration in 1964. A small window-access from the roof of the Friday Mosque was made in the masonry for access into the cavity and monitoring proposes which is still used today.

When we started to reconstruct the fallen parts of the two arches Sultan Fayaz proposed that we should use gypsum (plaster of Paris). At first we refused and explained about different kinds of lime mortar and their uses. But Sultan argued that the Ghurids had used gypsum and it was still used in Herat. He was right: Both Ghurids and Timurids had used this material and we saw a building site in Herat, where they glued the tiles on the walls with such mortar. In this way supports and moulds were unnecessary. Later on we observed that all of the decorations on the Ghurid portal were fixed in gypsum and maybe that was the only possible method.

When I thought about all these materials which were new to me: clay, clay bricks, ashes and gypsum then I did not feel as the experts in restoration as my contract read and I realized that the restoring of the monuments of Afghanistan would pose the scientist many new problems.

My contract with UNESCO finished and I had to return to Denmark before the work could be completed, but three months later I received a letter from Sharif which read as follows:

"We have all Ready Finish work of Herat Mosque on the April 17. and all we did to you order. We left Herat on April 25."

Sharif did not know one word of English one year before. ▪

Erik Hansen, 1965

Figure. 6.15: The team of architects, constructors, masons and laborers who worked on the project of restoration of the Ghurid Portal in Herat in 1964.

Baba Murad (a native of Faryab) and Sharif (a native of Mazar-i-Sharif) continued working for the Afghan department of monuments in Kabul and Balkh respectively, even after retirement. Sharif passed away at the age of 68 in May 2014. The other members of the team are also retired by now. ▪

Najimi, 2014

Figure 7.1: Remaining of the side wall decoration of the Ghurid Portal seen in 2013. The measurement inside the frame of the panel is 360 x 160 cm and then adding the 19 cm thickness of the frame makes it nearly 400 by 200 cm. Photo: Najimi, 2013.

CHAPTER 7

THE GHURID WALL DECORATIONS

ISLAMIC WALL DECORATION

Wall decoration on buildings has been part of the applied art and architecture in the Muslim world since long. Applied both at the interior and exterior surfaces of buildings, geometric patterns, floral and vegetal forms have made the main components of the surface ornamentation. In the pre 13th century Ghaznavid and Ghurid monumental buildings in Afghanistan decorations were built with exposed bricks in patterns that exhibited designs, and with the shadow lines created, it gave a three-dimensional effect.

THE GHAZNAVID DECORATIVE WORK

Imaginative use of brick for surface decoration work in Afghanistan was started with laying bricks in organized patterns on exposed facades as seen in the 10th and 11th Century buildings. The palace of Masud 3rd, east of the historic and walled town of Ghazni, was a site where many such elements of architectural decoration were found, characterized by the combination of baked brick with stucco (gypsum). The two remaining minarets in Ghazni are the best example of such works (figures 1.2, 1.3 and 7.2).

The masonry work of baked bricks embedded in a layer of mortar exhibit patterns and orders keeping the observers' eyes move continuously. The geometric designs created motifs like a woven work. *Girih*, a Persian word for "knot" has been known as a terminology for this interwoven pattern in decorations; and *girih sāzī* "knot making" or *girih chīnī* "arranging knots" have been known among the Persian speaking artisans working in the decorative designs. "Straight-edged symmetric shapes are used in *girih*. A *girih* typically consists of a strap work that form 6, 8, 10, or 12 pointed stars separated by polygons and straps, and often they are drawn in an interlacing manner. Such patterns usually consist of a repeating the "unit cell" with 2, 3, or 6 fold rotational symmetry that tiles the plane with no gaps." (Lee, A.J. (1987).

In places bricks are placed on edge (vertical) over a base course, some places specially produced or cut decorative bricks were used. The generated geometric patterns also constitute slots for embedding stucco elements in various sizes and shapes; some are characterizing vegetal decoration, others are geometric figures. The tiles are generally moulded and produced for a direct insertion into a designed slot (figure 5.4 b).

The colour of the bricks and stucco pieces would depend of what composition the clay may have; in some places it might be whitish yellow while another view might be a bit reddish yellow. A panel

Figure 7.2 (a , b): Detail of the minaret of Masud 3rd (a) and detail of the minaret of Bahram Shah (b) in Ghazni.

Figure 7.3 (a, b): Decorative pattern in brick work at Shah-i-Mashhad southern façade.(a) Photo: B. Glatzer, 1970. Sketch of a detail of 2nd layer of decorative masonry where some bricks are shaped on edges and laid differently as in Ghaznavid minarets and the Ghurid structure in Shah-i-Mashhad (b). Najimi, 2013.

found in situ in the audience chamber of the southern palace of Lashkari Bazaar, Helmand (figures 5.3 and 5.4 b) was made of fragments from stucco but bearing the same decorative features as that of geometric patterns and inlaid terracotta-tiles. This panel, now an exhibition in the National Museum in Kabul, suggests a substitution for elements of baked brick and stucco used during the Ghurid period.

Figure 7.4 (a, b): The Ghurid portal of the Chesht medressah, decorative work and text in terracotta. See translation on page 150.

Figure 7.5 (a, b): The Ghurid Minaret of Jam, decorative work in bricks and glazed elements

THE GHURID DECORATIVE WORK

The Ghurid builders in some way followed the style of construction and brick-based decorative techniques implemented by their predecessors. Despite the fact that many of the Ghurid buildings such as that of Chesht, Jam and Shah-i-Mashhad, were located close to mountains and rivers, which would have easily supplied stones as construction material, burned bricks actually made their main building material. Perhaps stone was used in foundations and infill of walls, but use of bricks would allow constructing in different thickness and geometric forms. The bricks also allowed for relatively rapid construction of arches and domes. The decorative panels implemented on Ghurid buildings were made of burned bricks. Architects and masons of Ghurid buildings used bricks with such a care and proficiency in creating delicate, intricate and interwoven forms that use of brick could ever offer. The terminology known in ornamental technique as *Hazarbaf* (Dhamija, Ram, 1975) – meaning a thousand inter-weaving – was commonly used for the intricate work of brick patterns such as that found on the minaret of Jam and the side wall of the Ghurid Portal in Herat Friday Mosque. Burned brick also provided the most suitable sub-structure of walls with gypsum plaster, which could be carved with decorative finishes in floral and geometric designs.

In 1964 Erik Hansen copied a number of the decorative designs, geometric as well as floral on parchment paper. Najimi has re-drawn the designs after the parchments and some of them are shown in the following (figures 7.6 (d), 7.8 (b), 7.10 (b), 7.12 (b), 7.15, and 7.22 (b, c, d)).

GEOMETRICAL PATTERNS OF TERRACOTTA

Designing the patterns of the brick decoration of the Ghurid Portal was in proportion to the size and thickness of the brick parts used. Bricks were either cut from larger sizes or elements were moulded in the desired shape before firing. In that case the parts can be designated terracotta parts rather than simply bricks.

As examples, four decorative pattern are explored by Najimi and Christensen on the following pages (figures 7.6-7.12). The idea was to re-create the different patterns by the use of three simple drafting tools: Compass, ruler and set square.

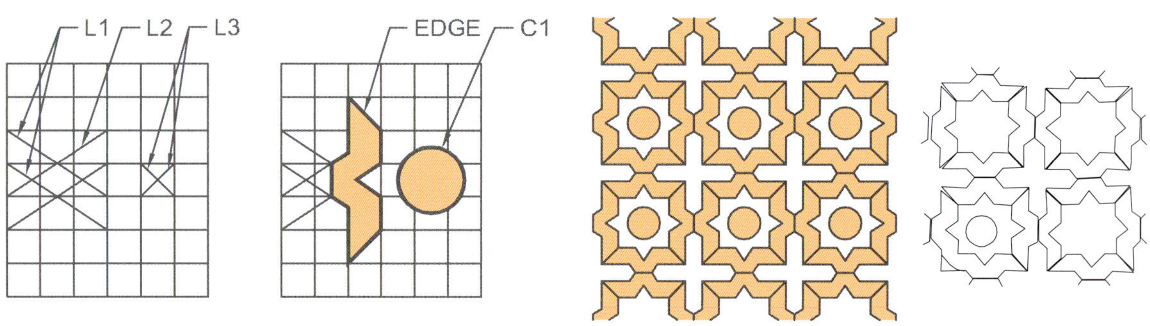

Figure 7.6 (a, b, c, d): Schematic drawing of a generic geometry leading to the detail of the terracotta decoration of the main arch at the Ghurid portal (figures 3.14, 6.6 and 7.14).

Figure a and b: Scale 1:5

- Draw a quadratic grid with grid distance = T where T is thickness of the terracotta part
- Draw the oblique guidelines L1, L2 and L3 as shown
- Draw the shape Edge using the intersections of grid lines and guidelines
- Draw the circle C1 with radius = T
- Array the shape Edge around the circle
- Copy the pattern to fill the available area

The design can be compared with figure d which is made from Erik Hansen's copy. Figure c and d: Scale 1:10.

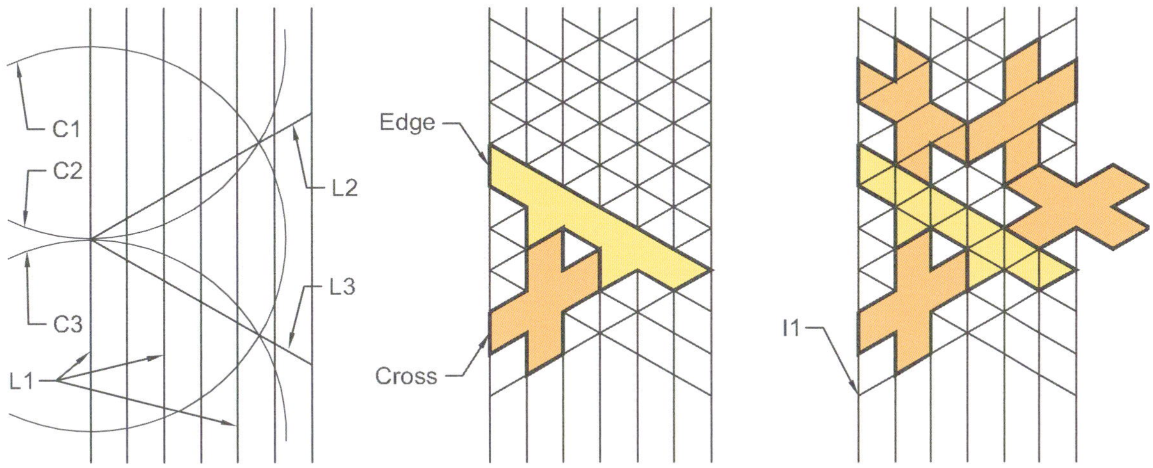

Figure 7.7 (a, b, c): Schematic drawing of a generic geometry leading to the terracotta detail on the façade of the Ghurid portal above the arch (figure 3.1). Scale 1:5.

- Draw 7 parallel lines L1 with distance equal to the thickness T of the terracotta elements
- Draw a circle C1 with center on the leftmost of the lines
- Draw circles C2 and C3 with centers in the intersections between the line and C1
- Use the intersections between C1, C2 and C3 to construct the two lines L2 and L3
- Draw an array of lines parallel to L2 and L3 with the distance T
- Use the triangular grid to draw the shape Edge and the X-shape
- Copy the X-shape 3 times on the other side of the Edge as shown
- Array the shape around the intersection I1

Figure 7.8 (a, b): On figure (a) the terracotta parts are coloured with different shades to make it easier to distinguish the pattern design. In reality the colour is the natural colour of the terracotta pieces. The design can be compared with figure b, made from Erik Hansen's copy. Scale 1:10.

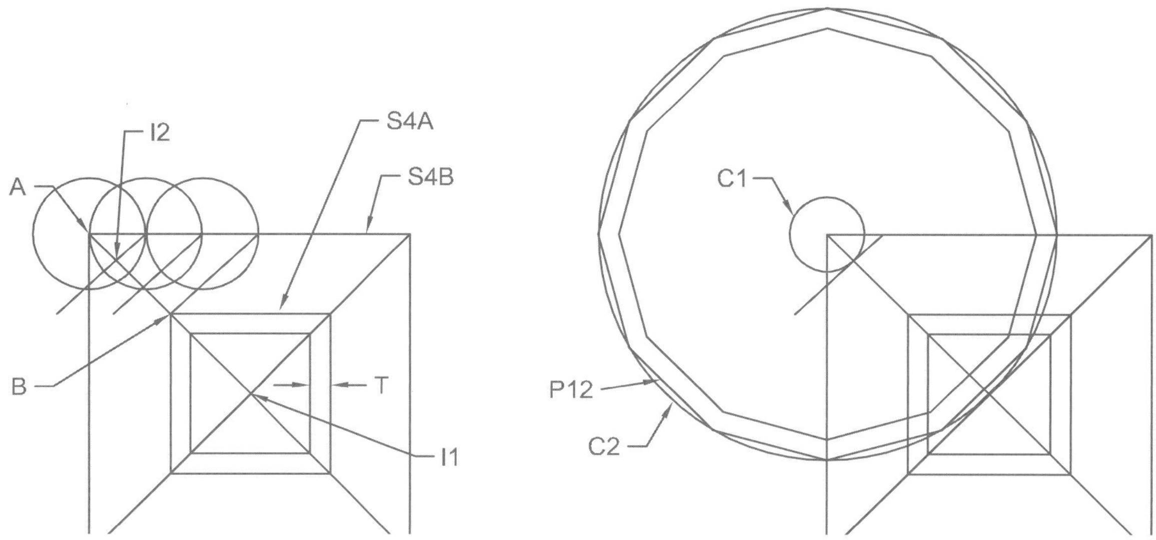

Figure 7.9 (a, b, c): (including opposite page) Schematic drawing of a generic geometry leading to the interlaced decorative work on the side-panels of the portal niche (figure 7.1). Scale 1:10.

- Draw a square, S4A with the side = 8T, where T is the thickness of the terracotta pieces. Add thickness T inside S4A.
- Draw a square, S4B around S4A in the distance 4T
- Draw the two diagonals in the squares. The intersection is designated I1
- Divide the distance between two corners, A and B of the two squares into three equally sized parts. The first intersection is designated I2
- Draw a circle, C1 with center in A and through I2
- Draw a circle, C2 with center in A and through I1
- Draw a 12 sided polygon, P12 inscribed in C2. Add thickness T inside P12

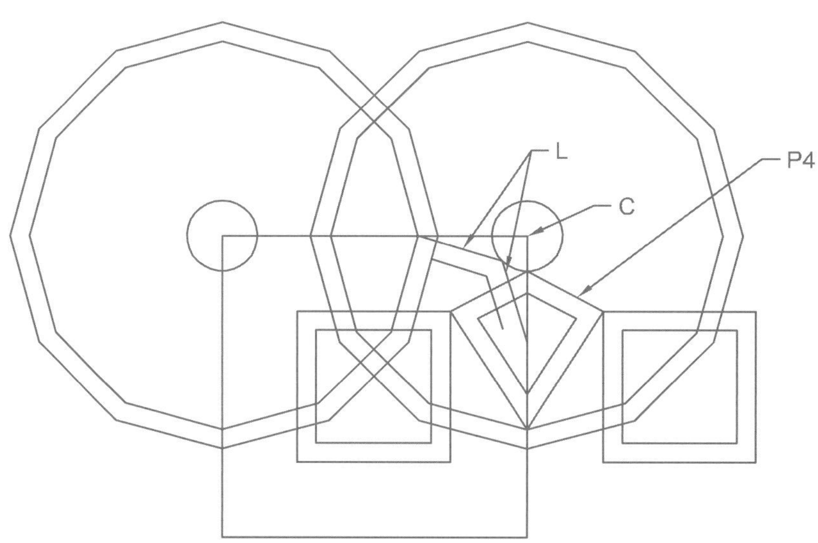

- Copy C1, S4A and P12 with thickness horizontally with the distance 16T (side length of S4B)
- Draw the kite-shaped polygon, P4 with 4 sides using the intersections and corners as shown. Add thickness T inside P4
- Copy the short sides, L of the kite-shape and rotate them 45° around C, the center of C3

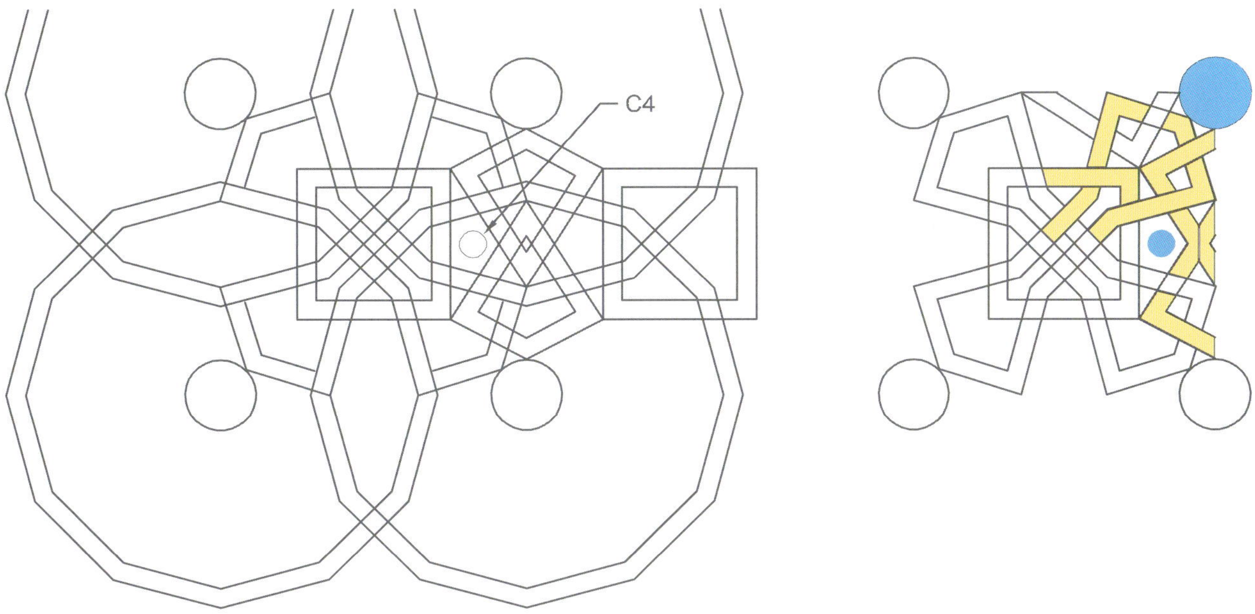

- Array L, P12, P4 (all including thickness) and C1 around I1. Join the lines L with polygons P12. Remove remaining parts of the P12 polygons
- Draw the circle C4 with diameter 1.5 x T in the middle of the pentagon
- Draw the terracotta pieces inside the pattern as shown. On the figure the pieces are reduced slightly in size to imitate the shrinkage of the drying terracotta

Figure 7.10 (a, b): By arraying (around I1) and copying of the terracotta pieces the final pattern is created The design can be compared with the figure to the right, made from Erik Hansen's copy. Scale 1:10.

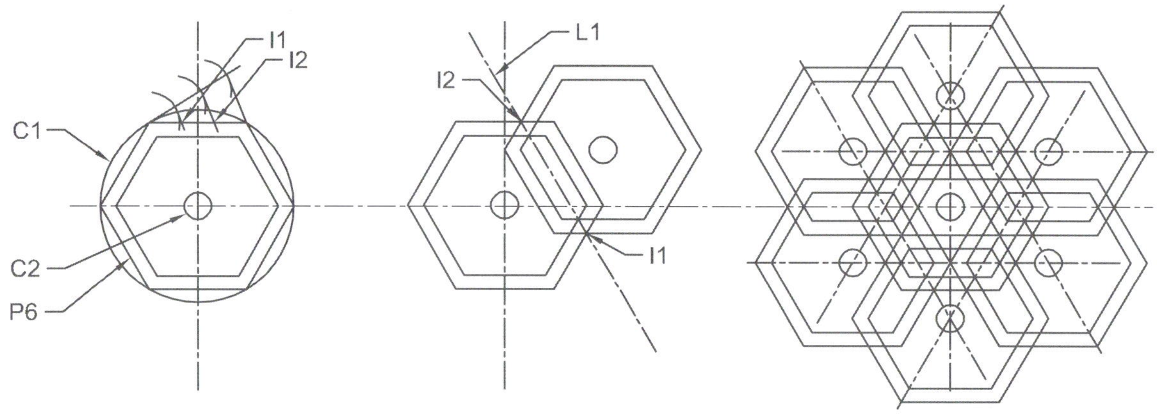

Figure 7.11 (a, b, c): Schematic drawing of a generic geometry leading to the detail of the soffit decoration of the main arch at the Ghurid portal (figure 3.15). Scale 1:10.

- Draw the circle C1 with radius = 7T where T is thickness of the terracotta part
- Draw the circle C2 with radius =T
- Draw the hexagon P6 inscribed in C1. Add thickness T inside P6
- Divide the sides of P6 in 3 equal sections by the points I1 and I2
- Draw a line L1 through I1 and I2 points of two sides of P6
- Mirror C2 and P6 with thickness in L1
- Repeat the mirroring for all 6 sides of P6
- Copy the pattern to fill the available area

Figure 7.12 (a, b): On figure a the terracotta parts are coloured with different shades to make it easier to distinguish the pattern design. In reality the colour is the natural colour of the terracotta pieces. The small circles C2 are glazed with blue glaze. The design can be compared with figure b, made from Erik Hansen's copy. Scale 1:10.

Figure 7.13: Detail of decoration in gypsum carving at the corners of the ceiling of the Ghurid Vault. Both floral motifs and other designs are carved in plaster that has also created structural shapes of corner arches on top of each other. The squinch below is decorated with terracotta pieces (figure 7.11).

FLORAL PATTERNS IN TERRACOTTA AND IN STUCCO

The soffit of the inner arch of the Ghurid vault is decorated by a floral band with narrow edges of geometric patterns (figures 6.5, 6.6 and 7.15). These terracotta parts are moulded in shape before firing. The same applies for the palmettos which sits behind the inscription on the façade and the floral design at the edge of the inscription (figures 3.7, 3.8 and 7.22).

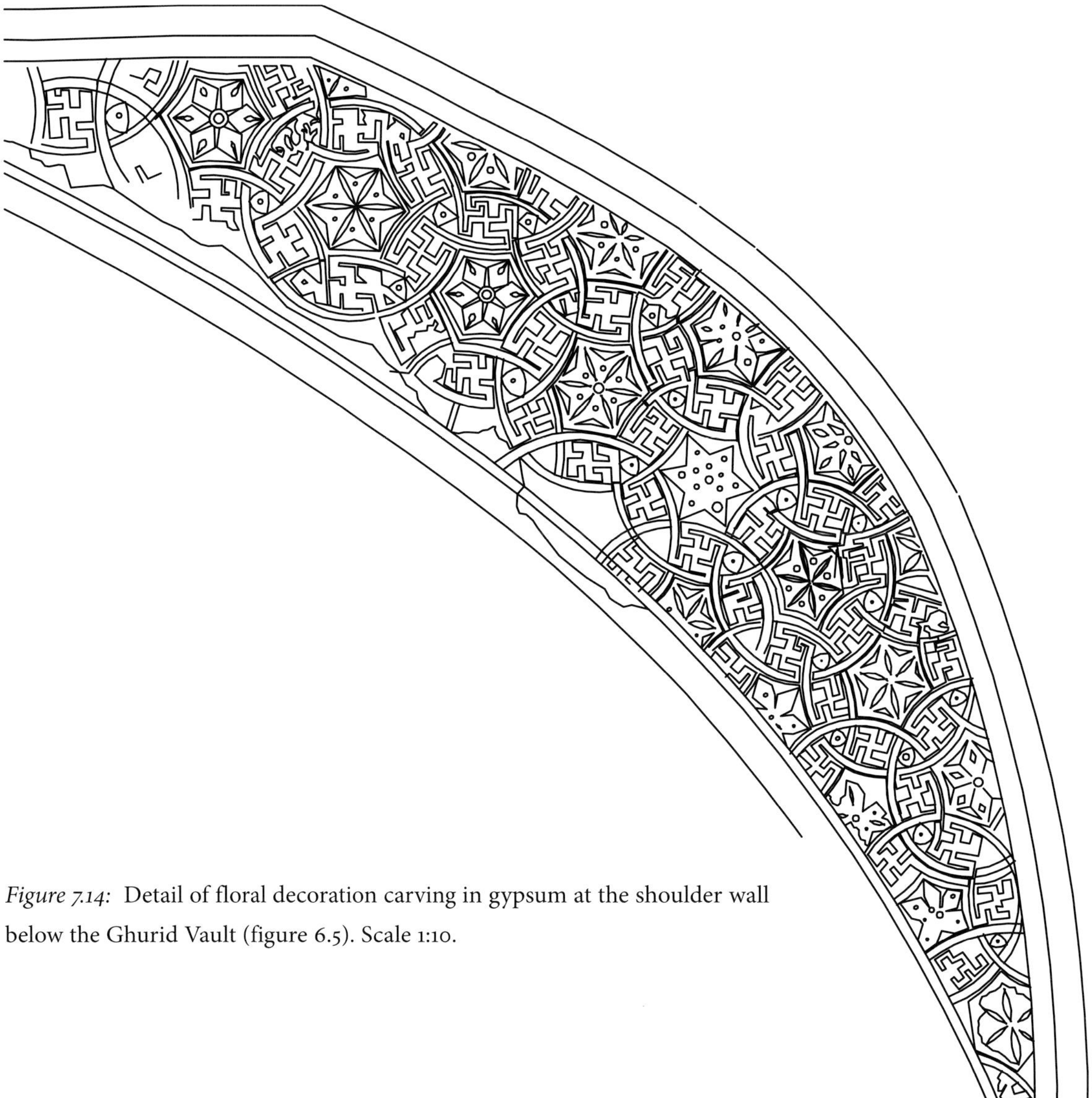

Figure 7.14: Detail of floral decoration carving in gypsum at the shoulder wall below the Ghurid Vault (figure 6.5). Scale 1:10.

Figure 7.15: Detail of the terracotta floral band running at the soffit of the inner arch. Drawn from Erik Hansen's copy. Scale 1:10.

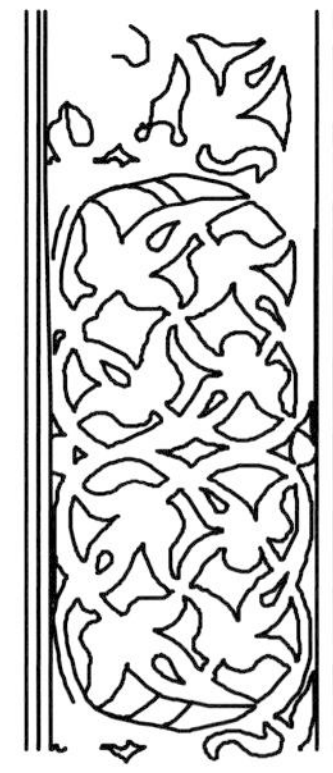

Figure 7.16: Gypsum carved framing of the Ghurid gate inside the Ghurid bay. Drawn based on photos of 1964. Scale 1:10.

Figure 7.17: Detail of decoration in gypsum carving at the joint line of the Ghurid Portal where floral motifs are continuously running as interwoven art work. Photo: Najimi, 2013.

Some of the decorations which are protected from rain and snow are carved in thick layers of gypsum plaster. At the corners of the ceiling of the Ghurid vault both floral motifs and other designs are carved in plaster that has also created structural shapes of corner arches on top of each other (figures 3.14 and 7.13).

A crescent shaped front of the inner arch (figures 6.5 and 7.14) is richly decorated with starlike geometric patterns.

A floral decoration of gypsum at the joint line of the niche was bordering the original entrance to the mosque (figures 7.16 and 7.17).

Figure 7.18: The brick work and terracotta decoration of the side wall of the Portal of Shah-i-Mashhad. Photo. B. Glatzer, 1993.

MESSAGE AND DECORATION

In addition to the geometric designs decorating the Ghurid buildings, calligraphic decoration also conveyed messages which were important to note. In the Islamic world, calligraphy has been considered one of the most important arts, also through the phases of children education. "Its role in recording the word of God in the Quran" (Jones, 1978) and communication has been obvious. Stylistic different and local variations in script have been used for calligraphically ornamented architecture.

All the Ghurids buildings we know had inscriptions. Two types were more common:

The Frontal inscription on portals were normally in Kufic style and made of bricks and terracotta moulded or cut pieces and normally bore the name and titles of the patron, the master builder and the date of ground breaking or completion of the construction. Remains of such inscriptions are still found on the buildings in Shah-i-Mashhad, Chesht, Jam and Herat.

The second type commonly applied inscriptions were created in gypsum work as horizontal bands inside the spaces of the mosques, madrassas and mausoleums. Content of such inscription were sometimes similar to that on the frontal inscriptions but more elaborate. Sometimes it also had contents and verses from Quran and Hadith.

The Ghurid sultans believing that victory was a divine help, decorated their buildings with text of chapter 48 of Quran, *Alfat'he* (the victory) and the *Sura Hasher v.22-24*. This too were made in both *Kufic* style, made of terracotta work as found in Shah-i-Mashhad, but also in gypsum work in *thulth* style as applied inside the Friday Mosque and the Sultan's mausoleum in Herat. One example is the inscription in figures 7.19 and 9.9. It has had as a lower layer yet another set of background cursive decoration.

Figure 7.19 (a, b): The Ghurid inscription inside southern Iwan of the Friday Mosque.
Photo a: Niedermayer, 1914. Photo b. Najimi, 2013.

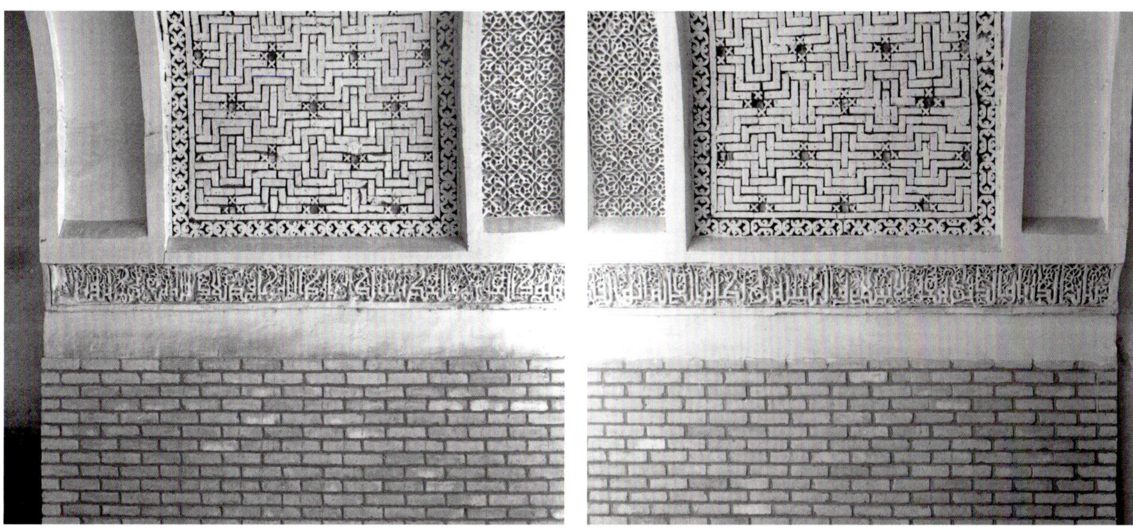

Figure 7.20 (a, b): The interior vaults at Friday Mosque of Herat bearing the Kufic gypsum inscription in praise of the Sultan Ghyath-ul-din.

In figure 7.19 (a, b) the Timurid corner pilaster and the glazed tile inscription at the courtyard facade are seen in Niedermayer's photo of 1914. Part of the inscription's beginning is not visible today as it got covered by the brick pillar of the archway constructed in 1944-50.

INSCRIPTION DOCUMENTS THE MOSQUE BEING GHURID

Prior to revealing of the inscription on the Ghurid Portal in 1964, the inscriptions still found in the vaults at the western iwan of the Friday Mosque (figure 7.20) and at interior of the mausoleum documented that the structure was a Ghurid building. Stuckert (1942), Chirvani (1970) reported that the inscription inside the main iwan of the Friday Mosque of Herat was:

Figure 7.21 (a, b): Horizontal band of inscription made in gypsum on interior wall of the medressah in Chesht-i-Sharif. See translation on page 150.

السلطان المعظم، شهنشاه الاعظم، مالک رقاب الامم مولی ملوک العرب و العجم
سلطان الارض الله حافظ بلاد الله معین خلیفه.... غیاث الدنیا و الدین معز الاسلام
و المسلمین ابو الفتح محمد بن سام قسیم امیر المومنین انار الله بر هانه

Translation: *The exalted Sultan, the greatest king of kings, who have followers of nations, master of the territories of the Arabs and non-Arabs the Sultan of God's earth, the protector of God's lands, the supporter of the Caliph of. ... He who succours the world and the faith, who strengthens Islam and the Muslims, ruler of Victorious Muhammad b. Sam, deputy Amir of the Believers, may God illuminate his rule.*

INSCRIPTION OF THE GHURID PORTAL

The Ghurids initiated the use of enamelled turquoise blue bricks and floral elements that were used for making of decorative Kufic inscriptions, which was applied to both the minaret of Jam and the Ghurid portal at the Friday Mosque of Herat. The portal inscriptions in Chesht and Shah-i-Mashhad were similar in technique but were not glazed.

The translation of the Kufic inscription can be found on page 94.

The words on the crown of the portal, which had fallen earlier, could not be read. With help of reading the gypsum-bed remains of the added Timurid tile layer and in reference to the gypsum inscription inside the main iwan Seljooki (1964) and Rejayee (1982) came up with a proposals for the missing text.

In the Appendix Najimi has attempted a reconstruction of the Ghurid portal based on the available information. ▪

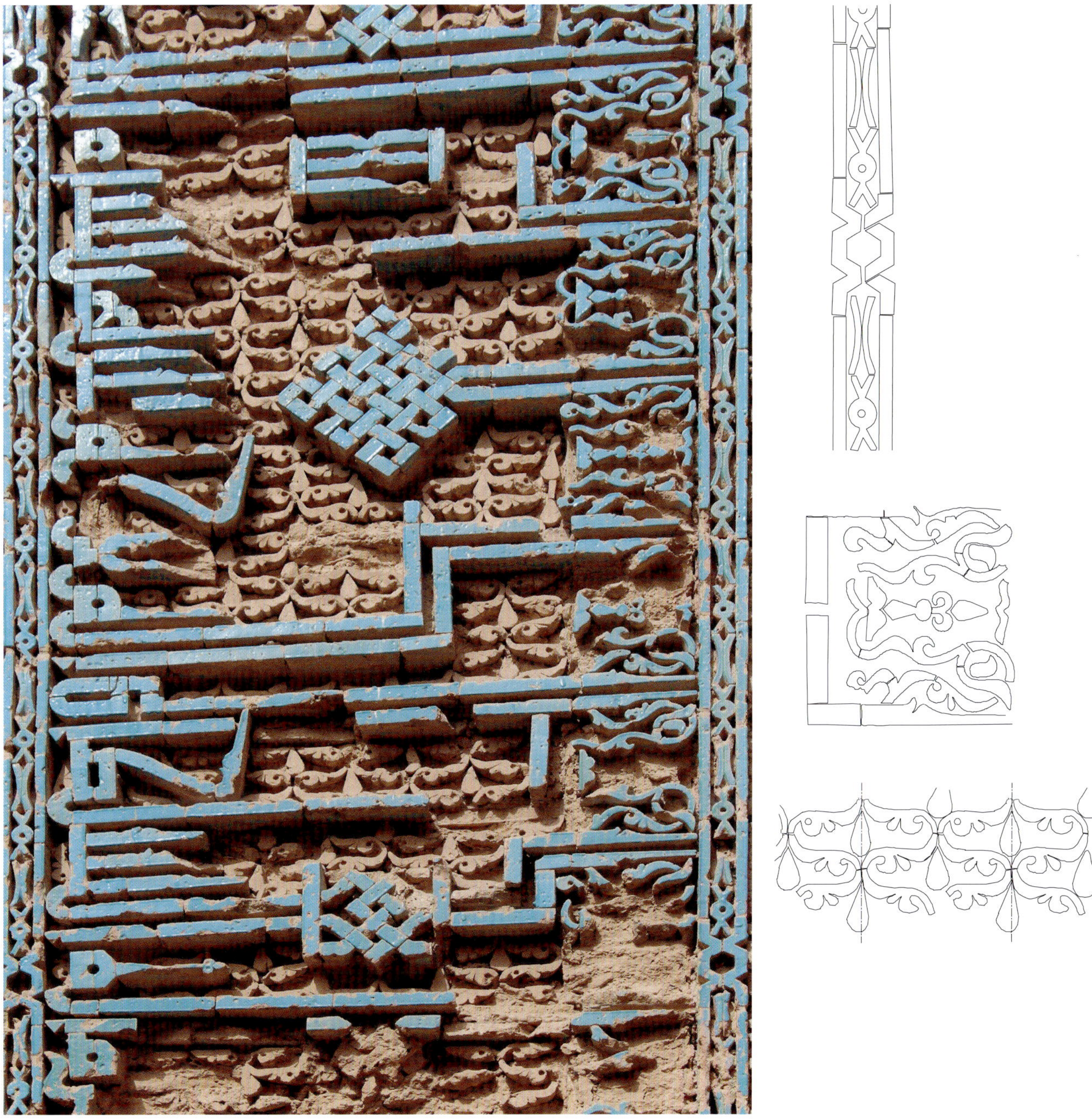

Figure 7.22 (a, b, c, d): Details of the glazed inscription on the Ghurid Portal.

(a) Photo: Najimi, 2013

(b) Detail of glazed terracotta elements making the frame of the Kufic inscription

(c) Detail of the glazed brick making floral design at the glazed inscription panel

(d) Detail of the terracotta palmettos which forms the background of the great inscription. The terracotta has small spots of glazing

(b), (c) and (d) are made from Erik Hansen copies on parchment paper. Scale 1:10.

Figure 8.1: The monochrome tiles medallions sat in baked brick framing applied by Timurids on the minarets of the Ghawarshad complex in Herat.. Photo: Najimi, 2013.

CHAPTER 8

THE TIMURID WALL DECORATIONS

HISTORY OF TILES

While we know that the Ghurids applied glaze on solid bricks that were used for creating the portal inscriptive decoration, we also know that the Timurids further developed use of glazed tiles for surface decoration in their buildings as discussed in chapter two to five. The history of tiles in the region, we learn, originates from the pre-Islamic period. Tiles were used in the temple of Choga Zanbil in Khuzistan, in the 13th century B.C. Square tiles made of baked clay, painted with red geometrical designs, were found in Luristan at Baba Jan Tepe belonging to the eighth century B.C. (Carboni and Masuya, 1993). The Achaemenids (550-330 BC) used glazed and decorated fired bricks in yellow, green and brown on the palaces of Susa and Persepolis. The Sassanid's used thinner (one centimetre thick) tiles for decorative purposes that had mosaic patterns of flowers, plants, geometric designs, birds and human figures. "Excavations in Firouzabad and Bishapour (today's Iran) have yielded evidence of tile art and mosaic manufacture for the Sassanid period" (History of Iranian Tile, 2013).

In the Islamic period, tile work was used in Mesopotamia in the mid-ninth century, but in Islamic Persia and Khurasan tile production became known in the eleventh century. Such early tile ware was recorded in excavations in Ghazni, palace of Masud, at the post Ghaznavid layer dated to the early 13th century (Carboni and Masuya, 1993).

As architects we are interested to know that the earliest use of tilework on architectural surfaces was believed to have been found on the minaret of the Friday Mosque in Damghan of 1058. It was an inscriptional frieze in turquoise-glazed tiles making a horizontally run Kufic inscription.

The composition of turquoise tiles, on external walls, as mosaic components of geometrical patterns in contrast with the yellow / reddish surface of baked bricks appeared like jewels.

During the rule of Seljuks in early thirteenth century, Kashan was the major producer of tiles and glazed pottery. Therefore, the term *Kashi,* also used in Afghanistan today, was referred to the glazed pottery with style from Kashan. Wall decorative tiles were produced in shapes of pentagon, hexagon, octagon and as stars of three, five, six and eight points – stamped or painted over and glazed, which originally was known as *minayee* (glazed), later also known as *haftrangi* (seven-colored) in the period between the mid-twelfth and the early thirteenth centuries. Some tiles were glazed in cobalt blue, the Lapizlozid locally known as *lajward*, in Persia such tile production was known as the *liijvardinah* that appeared in the 13th century until the midfourteenth century (Carboni and Masuya, 1993).

Tile production developed again between the second half of the fourteenth century (Ilkhanid) and in the fifteenth century, Timurids applied it to the major buildings in their empire.

Figure 8.2: Remaining of a 15th century Timurid tile work in the Friday Mosque of Herat, where bricks are used for demarcation of the geometric network of shapes the tiles are placed in. Photo: Najimi, 2013.

THE TIMURID TILES

During the Timurid periods glazed tile became the most important decorative feature of the religious and monumental structures. The 15th century cities of Herat and Samarkand, among others, had the best tile work in the style of *kashi-moaraq* (inlaid mosaic tile). This type of tile was produced from assembling pieces, geometric or floral, cut and carved from baked glazed tiles (10 cm x 10 cm) of different colours (figures 8.7-8.15).

The body of a tile-brick was painted over with emulsion containing pigments of silver and copper, and then it was fired a second time. Pre-cut tiles were produced in turquoise and cobalt blue, black, green, burnt orange (golden) and white glaze. The emulsion came from plants and powders of metallic elements and oxides, and attained their maximum brilliance when baked in smaller mud ovens using hard wood for fuel (to have less smoke). Melting temperatures for the applied glaze varied in range from 800°C for lead glazes, to 1600°C for tin and cobalt.

To produce a designed mosaic panel, the Timurid artists laboriously cut out – chiselled off and adjusted each piece by hand, each fragment in desired colour according to a previously prepared design. When finished the pieces were put upside down on a design sketched on the type of surface required (flat, curved, concave etc.). The tile cutting allowed for gaps to cavities for gypsum-sand plaster to

Figure 8.3: The 15th century built ceiling of the Timurid vault at the Ghurid Portal restored in 1964, Photo: Najimi, 2013. This photo could be compared with figure 4.7. The reader may note that the structure has been in stable condition since its restoration half a century ago.

be poured over them and making a panel often reinforced with reeds. The plaster was left to dry and hardened before the panel could be moved for installation.

When a decorative mosaic panel was ready to be installed, mainly on the exterior walls, in some cases at interior Mihrabs of mosques, the panels sat about an inch away from the wall surface, the gap was filled in by a gypsum-sand grout. The gypsum mortar hardened quickly. The gypsum mixed with sand allowed the plaster to breathe during different seasons and levels of air humidity.

"An interesting point was that the mosaic tile was not stuck on the smooth brick plastered surface at dead level. It was stuck on at a slightly undulating level so that with the changing light and reflections, the brilliance of the colours created new hues and new colour blends. Colours were used in striking accents or in gentle variations, and were often employed to cover an entire monument including walls, niches, domes and interiors as well as exteriors" (Dhamija, Ram 1975).

MIXED TILE AND BRICK DECORATIONS

While glazed tile was the main decorative tradition of the Timurid builders, they also followed on the Ghurid tradition to create geometric patterns in bricks, mixing the two traditions. They mastered a popular technique of creating designs of glazed medallions sat in the brick framing. (figs. 8.1-8.4) Also

Figure 8.4: Close up of the glazed medallion and use of glazed pointing between baked bricks, at the Timurid vault of the Ghurid Portal. Photo: Najimi, 2013.

thin bricks with coloured glazing were used together with unglazed bricks (figures 8.3 and 8.4). This type of decoration was used in religious and nonreligious buildings from the 13th century onwards both by the Timurids and later by others (History of Iranian Tile, 2013). The Timurid work on the Ghurid portal also have some examples of this.

Calligraphy still had an important place in the decorative works produced in tile production. In addition to *thulthe* style of calligraphy the Timurids also introduced a style named *Nastalique* that were first applied for inscription on buildings, but later also for books. Calligraphy, like all Islamic decorations, is linked to artistic geometry and has mathematically understood visual proportions. Inscriptions were mostly used as a frame along the edges of the main and most visible openings of the buildings. Externally they decorated portals and cornices. At the interior inscriptions run like a horizontal or aligned band at a height above the openings. Sometimes single words or phrases were also arranged in repetitive manner in a band of Kufic or other styles, or a geometric shape, emphasizing a message.

Little of the Timurid tiled inscription were remaining on the facade of the Ghurid portal and the pieces were not complete enough to allow reading or guessing the content of the full inscription by the Timurids (fig. 8.6). This detail was on the left pillar of the portal and should be read from top downwards. Apart from white, only three colours – green, blue and golden – were used which was the

Figure 8.5: Detail of the glazed tiles in the Timurid tile work on the south side wall of the Ghurid portal. The photo shows the tiles when half of them had been cleaned with water.

style of the time. Those pieces were taken down both for revealing the Ghurid inscription and to store the Timurid remains in Herat museum in 1964.

Unable to read its content we asked a few Afghan calligraphers, who suggested that it could have been a poetry from Saa'di, as his poems were also found in the mosque of Ghalwar, west of Herat city, also a Timurid construction. (Najimi, 2009).

An example of *kashi-haft-rangi* tiles (of star shape) mixed with unglazed brick was also applied by the Timurids on the Ghurid portal, framing the timurid inscription. (figs. 4.2., 6.2 and 6.3).

Figure 8.6: Detail of remaining of Timurid tiled inscription (15th C.) that was covering the Ghurid glazed inscription of the portal.

Figure 8.7: Clay brought form a hillside quarry is cleaned and mixed with water. After a day the watersaturated mud is cast into tile bricks – square format of about 10 centimeter and two centimeter thick. A day or two later the bricks are turned on edge to get dry from both sides.

THE POST TIMURID ERA TILE WORK

The Safavid artists followed the Timurid tradition and later on added two more colours to the art of glazing tiles: yellow and light blue. They also simplified the production of glazed tiles so that more wall space could be decorated in lesser time.

For putting emulsion of different pigments on the same tile plate, a buffer line was drawn first, a technique know as *euerda seea* technique (Carboni and Masuya, 1993). While known earlier, it was widely used in the Safavid period (16th to 17th centuries). In Herat and Balkh it has been known as *kashi-haft-rangi*, (seven colours). Unlike the *kashi-moaraq* tiles that are composed of cut pieces, working with the *kashi-haft-rangi* style square tiles plates arranged together and each one therefore painted to produce a decorative larger panel of geometric and figural designs. The dark lines of the *cuerda seca* replace the black outlines, while the palette is large though usually set on a dull yellowish-green background.

Traditionally the tile producer could not measure the temperature of the oven for baking glazed tiles, but they have judged visually from melting of the tile glaze. Today we learn that "the *haft-rangi* tiles however are normally baked at about 1050° C uniformly, for all the colours, some colours therefore did not achieve their maximum brilliance." (Dhamija, Ram 1975).

Figure 8.8: The dry bricks are baked in the large kiln.

Photo: Figures 8.8-8.11: C. Christensen, 1971.

Figure 8.9: After application of liquid glaze emulsion (figures 8.10 and 8.11) the tiles are baked again in another kiln with the temperature required for the glaze to melt.

Figure 8.10: Production of material for glazing: Oven for making of lead ash. The lead is extracted from old car batteries. The mortar is used for crushing of quartz and glass.

Figure 8.11: Hand grinder for glazing emulsion made from water, lead ash, quartz and soda or from crushed glass.

Figure. 8.12 (a, b, c, d): For producing *kashi-moaraq* the skilled masters cut shapes out from the glazed bricks, following the design – geometric, floral or for inscriptions (figure 8.12 a-d). Each piece has undercut sides, which gives place for the gypsum mortar used to glue the pieces together.
Floral sub-patterns are pre-assembled using gypsum on the rear side. In figure 8.12 c the craftsman is holding such sub-patters in his hands. The cut elements of the various colored shapes are arranged in reverse on the sketch of the design. Photo: Figure 8.12 c: C. Christensen, 1971.

As mentioned in chapter two, a tile production for the maintenance of the facades of the Friday Mosque was re-established in the 1940s. This workshop in the Friday Mosque still follows both the *moaraq* and *haft-rangi* tradition for the tiles they produce for the repair works. While the artisans follow old designs, they also practice some simple patterns . Elder masters have also been training younger pupils through apprenticeship.

Figure 8.13: Once all pieces are arranged completing the design, a layer of mortar of gypsum plaster is cast over to produce a mosaic panel in transportable size and possible to install on the wall (figure 8.15). This finished panel of tiled mosaic is intended for installation at top of an arch way. The trace of the pattern is also seen on the floor on which the panel was produced in the workshop of the Friday Mosque in 1964.

The cutting tools used in the *moaraq* tile workshops are simple and traditional: A blacksmith forges hammers, chisels, drills and files, using scrap steel from e.g. lorry springs as raw material. The blacksmith knows the art of hardening the steel and also how to cut files with a chisel while the steel is soft followed by hardening.

The figures 8.7-8.15 show the production process of *kashi-moaraq* from the raw clay to fixing of the finished panel on the building. Figures 8.16-8.18 show the *haft-rangi* process. ▪

Figure 8.14: Curved tile sections can be made by using curved templates: The craftsman is placing details on such a curved template.
Photo: Figures 8.14 and 8.15: C. Christensen, 1971.

Figure 8.15: The finished panel is mounted on the mosque wall. The scaffolding is made of poplar wood connected with iron bands from wooden transport crates.

Figure 8.16: Haft-rangi tile production: Baked square tiles of 15 x 15 centimetres are placed together and the necessary design (full panel) is drawn on them as dark buffer lines.
Each part of the pattern is painted by the emulsion for the desired colour.
They still produce in designs composed of yellow, blue, brown, black, turquoise, green and white.
Photo: Najimi, 2013.

Figure 8.17: The craftsman is applying the emulsion between the black buffer lines. After drying the tiles go to an oven to be glazed. The basic constituents of the emulsion used must be the same, only the pigment differs. Otherwise it is not possible to bake all colours at the same temperature.
Photo: Najimi, 2013.

Figure 8.18: A panel of tiles with inscription in *thulth* style made by the *Haft-rangi* method.
Photo: C. Christensen. 2005.

Figure 9.1: The inside of the portal dome of the Madrassa in Chesht is an example of typical Ghurid work in brick masonry and decorative work produced in bricks and terracotta using gypsum mortar.

CHAPTER 9

MASONRY, MORTAR AND PLASTER

The reader of this book will have seen from previous chapters the many fine examples of architectural monuments made from simpler material, such as clay, clay bricks and baked brick using clay, lime or gypsum as constituent in mortar and plaster.

In this chapter we will describe these materials, how they are produced and how they were used a long time ago up until present day.

CLAY WALLS (*PAKHSA*)

The solid walls of most of the historic structures in Afghanistan have been made directly from clay mud in a thickness of 60 cm to 125 cm. Such a wall is called *pakhsa.* The building of the *Pakhsa* was found to be much easier when clay from the site itself could be used. The mud is prepared by soaking clay with water for some days. Stone or burned bricks are used for the foundation and to protect the wall against damage from melting snow or flowing water in the spring.

Workers pile the soft mud on the foundation by shovels. Each row of *pakhsa* are raised some 60-70 cm and left to dry for some days. Then the sides are cut to shape while still wet to give them a straight and smooth surface and the next layer can be piled up. At some intervals flat stones or timber are added in the corners for lateral reinforcements, as the dry mud has very little tensile strength. *Pakhsa* wall is most often used for the construction of the ground floor only, while sun dried bricks have commonly been used for constructions of the second floor and higher, as wall thickness can be reduced and transportation of bricks is easier than the wet mud.

CLAY BRICKS (*KHISHT-E-KHOM*)

Sun-dried clay bricks are also used as building material for finished buildings. The bricks are made by moulding wet clay in a wooden frame (similar to figure 8.7). The bricks are dried in the sun so they become stable, but not necessarily until they are completely dry.

In Herat area common houses are made with 4 thick corner pillars of clay brick using mud as mortar. The pillars are connected by arches made on a scaffold or by short timber, often merely branches of wood. The roof is made as a dome which can be built without any scaffolding because the flat bricks, typically 25 x 25 x 5 cm can be glued in place by the mud mortar and will stick long enough for the mason to close a stable circle or spiral of bricks. This would hardly be possible if the bricks had a format similar to the bricks used in the west. Finally the walls and especially the roof is covered with a mixture of clay and straw, *kah-gel.*

Figure 9.2: Workers making a garden wall of *pakhsa* near the village of Qashshah south-east of Herat. Photo: C. Christensen, 2002.

CLAY PLASTER WITH STRAW (*KAH-GEL*)

Clay plaster is prepared several days before use. The clay is soaked by water to make it very soft. Straw is mixed into the clay by workers walking in the mud. The process is repeated for several days until the plaster is homogeneous and easy to apply to straighten the walls indoors and outdoors, and to tighten the roof.

Archaeological evidence indicates that both mortar and plaster made of mud-straw was used as early as four thousand years BC.

This type of plaster is stronger than pure clay plaster because the straw acts as reinforcement of the clay. The plaster insulates for heat and absorbs sound. The straw also inhibits, though not prevents, the rain in washing away the clay. Water is carefully drained away from the roof through wooden gutters projecting from the walls, but snow is dangerous because it may soak the clay during a long melting period. To prevent this the house owners will clear the roof of snow, which will then become a threat to the lower parts of the outer walls unless they have water resistant foundations of stone or burned bricks set in strong mortar.

As long as the walls and especially the roof of a clay building are properly maintained they can last for centuries but the constant adding of clay on the roof can endanger the building stability due to the extra weight (figures 6.11 and 6.12).

When a building has been abandoned then rain and snow will deteriorate the structure and the water penetrating into the building structure can do great damage, as the restoration team found on the Ghurid portal.

Figure 9.3: Brick kiln in Injil south of Herat. Photo: C. Christensen, 1974.

BURNT BRICK (*KHISHT-E-PUKHTEH*)

To provide protection against rain and snow, burnt bricks were often used as the exterior layer of the wall and the roof while pakhsa or sun-dried bricks made the rest in some structures in the region. Hard baked large size bricks were used for foundations in places where stone was not available. Bricks from the Ghazni historical sites measures 43 x 22 x 8 cm, 40 x 40 x 5 cm and 22 x 22 x 5 cm. Bricks from the Ghurid wall foundations and floor pavement measures 30 x 30 x 5 cm but burnt bricks in size of 22 x 22 x 5 cm have also been used for the Ghurid and Timurid constructions.

Plain burnt bricks made a solid background for the gypsum mortar which glues the decorative elements on monumental structures having clay walls. The decorative elements were made from carefully selected bricks with sharp corners or even from bricks with decorative shapes (figure 7.3).

Some clay details moulded into complex shapes before the burning, as we have seen on the side panels of the Ghurid portal (figure 3.11), are better designated as terracotta details than simply as bricks.

Many important structures in the monumental buildings with arches, domes and vaults were made exclusively from burned brick in order to obtain the necessary strength and durability (e.g. figure 9.1).

Although mud mortar or mud mortar with straw was used together with burned brick in many buildings, better mortar with lime or gypsum was a better choice to obtain resistance against weathering.

MORTAR

Mortar is used to fill the spaces between the uneven surfaces of bricks and to hold the bricks together. Mortar acts as construction element that distributes the load from the building above and transfers the force to the lower part of the structure without breakage of the bricks.

The mortar should be able to penetrate the surface of the adjoining parts and glue them together immediately to keep the bricks in place. This is especially important when building arches or domes. After hardening it must have sufficient strength to join the bricks to an integrated structure but it should also be elastic to allow for thermal expansion of the bricks.

As mentioned above mud made from clay and water can be used as mortar and it is well suited as mortar for sun-dried bricks. For burned bricks a better mortar is justified both to have higher tensile strength and to give the mortar resistance comparable to the bricks against weathering.

To produce such mortar at least two substances are needed: The adhesive and the filler. The substances used traditionally have been burned lime or gypsum as adhesive and clay, sand and ash as filler. The following sections will discuss how these two adhesives were produced in Afghanistan and examples of their use.

MORTAR WITH BURNED LIME (*AHAK*)

Lime kilns are used to convert local limestone ($CaCO_3$) into burned lime (CaO), which is then treated with water to form hydrated lime, ($Ca(OH)_2$), in the following simply called lime.

Mixed on situ, mortar of mud and lime makes a base good for compressive force, mostly used for adding strength to the bottom of foundations. Softer grounds are strengthened by the use of this mixture. For each cubic meter of soil between 100 to 300 kg lime is applied.

The lime mortar will harden due to a chemical reaction between carbon dioxide (CO_2) from the air and the hydrated lime in the mortar, which is turned back into limestone:

$$Ca(OH)_2 + CO_2 \rightarrow CaCO_3 + H_2O$$

Higher strength can be achieved by adding some sand or gravel or by using lime and sand only as is common in the west.

A very strong and waterproof mortar called *sarooj* or *sandalla* is made from lime, sand and ash (from burning wood). The mixture of water and the constituents must be thoroughly beaten for a couple of days before so the particles of different sizes forms a very dense matrix, which is waterproof. *Sarooj* is commonly used for foundations of important buildings and for surfaces that must be waterproof, like in a bath, h*amam* and in water cisterns.

Although lime mortar is well known in Afghanistan gypsum is more common as adhesive in mortar and in plaster for indoor use as we shall see in the following section. The very common use of gypsum as adhesive was surprising to Erik Hansen, because lime is far more commonly used for mortar in the west (page 100) where gypsum is also known as plaster of Paris or stucco.

GYPSUM (*GACH*)

The production and use of gypsum as building material has been known for very long. Remains of stucco and gypsum from more than 2500 years ago was found at archaeological sites of the Achaemenid period of Persia.

Gypsum stone is found in many places in Afghanistan, as deposits in the mountains (figure 9.4). The stone is soft and can be quarried by simple tools.

The chemical formula for gypsum stone is $CaSO_4$, $2H_2O$. The water is bound as crystal water. Heating it to about 110 to 130°C will remove most of the crystal water so it becomes $CaSO_4$, $0.5H_2O$.

Figure 9.4 (a, b): Gypsum quarry near Rabat Sabcheh. Photo: C. Christensen, 1974.

The hardening takes place when water is added and bound as crystal water again, a much faster process than hardening of lime mortar. While the burning of lime involves a chemical reaction, the baking of gypsum is a physical reaction which requires less energy.

The baking was made in a simple kiln (figures 9.5 and 9.6). The stones are stacked into the kiln and wood or straw are fired from below. The simple design of the kiln does not permit accurate temperature control. If the baking temperature is less than desired then the produced gypsum loose less water and therefore remains hard. If the gypsum stone is heated too much all of the crystal water is removed turning the gypsum into "dead burned" gypsum, which only bind crystal water again very slowly and therefore can become nearly useless.

The outer shell of the baked stones of gypsum will be more dehydrated than its core part. After cooling the baked stones are crushed and sieved. The most dehydrated parts, locally known as "dead gypsum", separates as fine powder while the inner core, locally known as "active gypsum", remains in larger pieces and must be crushed a second time.

By repeatedly crushing and sieving the gypsum it can be separated into two or three fractions which can all be used for different purposes, as described in the following sections.

It is said that the best gypsum lump is the one having blue "sapphire" rings, perhaps from being heated slowly in the kiln by low heat. In that case the inner half-baked part of the lump is supposed to be better for mortar and plaster works in buildings.

Figure 9.5: Gypsum kiln in Rabat Sabcheh near Herat. Photo: C. Christensen, 1974.

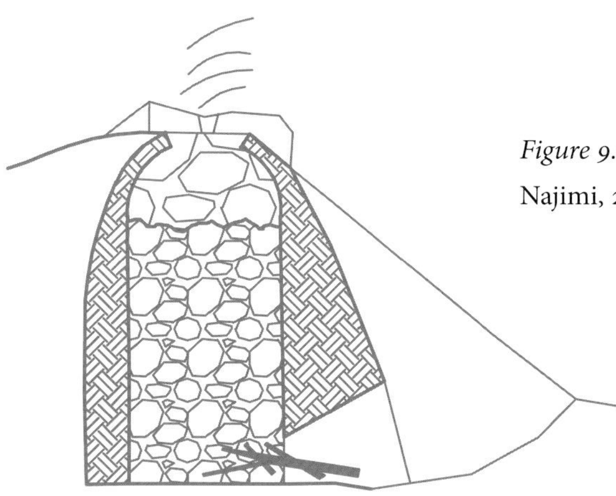

Figure 9.6: Sketch of cross section of gypsum kiln. Najimi, 2013.

CLAY-GYPSUM MORTAR (*KHAK-GACH*)

Clay-gypsum mortar is prepared from clay or soil as filler and from active gypsum. The soil is sieved as only very fine particles will give a good result. The soil powder is mixed with the gypsum powder in volume ratios between 2:1 to 1:1.

Figure 9.7 (a, b): A local worker is preparing the wet gypsum plaster for the mason (see figure next page).
Photo: Najimi, 2013.

This mixture is poured into a wide jar with water in the volume ratio 1:2 and mixed rapidly, less than a minute with the water. The mortar must be used immediately as it hardens fast. This type of mortar is commonly used in wall, arch and dome constructions.

Although the clay-gypsum mortar is more resistant to weathering than pure clay mortar, it must be protected from the direct influence of rain and snow. Because of this a dome from burned bricks and clay-gypsum mortar must be protected either by a layer of *kah-gel* or with burned bricks set in water proof *sarooj* mortar.

Gypsum is also used alone without filler as mortar and plaster in various forms such as finalplaster of wall surface and pouring grout behind tiled panels setting on walls. The following sections describe the names, preparation and use of such mixtures.

IMMEDIATE GYPSUM PLASTER (*GACH-I-DESTI*)

This plaster is mixed from active gypsum and water only. The fine gypsum powder is spread on the water surface and mixed rapidly. As soon as the mix has become a paste it must be used because it becomes hard within 10 minutes. Such plaster is normally used for manufacturing of embossed and carved decorations (figures 9.9) reliefs and framings on the wall surfaces as well as grouting behind tiles. Immediate gypsum mix is the strongest type of gypsum mortar.

WET GYPSUM PLASTER (*GACH-I-KHISIDA*)

The wet gypsum plaster contains, as the name implies, relatively more water in relation to gypsum than the immediate gypsum plaster. This results in a plaster, which hardens relatively slower and which is very suitable for plastering walls, which has been flattened by *kah-gel* plaster .

The fine gypsum powder is spread on the water surface and mixed for two minutes. When the gypsum has absorbed the water, whereby it expands and becomes pasty, the paste is cut into blocks, which can be applied for plastering.

Figure 9.8: The mason is applying the finishing layer of wet gypsum plaster to a gypsum-mud plastered wall.
Photo: Najimi, 2013.

If warm water is used for the mix, the plaster will be quick to harden. In cases where a slow adhesion process of a gypsum product is desired 7 to 10 percent lime can be added to delay the hardening for 10 to 15 minutes. Small amounts (0.2%) of plant glue powder can also be used for this effect.

DISSOLVED GYPSUM PLASTER

Adhesion of this type of plaster is something between the immediate gypsum plaster and that of the wet gypsum plaster. It contains even more water relative to gypsum than wet gypsum plaster and the best quality of gypsum is used.

The gypsum powder is spread on the water surface and dissolved into the water. After a minute the plaster is mixed again for a minute. After resting a minute the paste is put on a trowel and applied as final plaster on the wall surfaces. It is possible to apply up to 7 or 8 mm thick plaster using this method.

KILLED GYPSUM PASTE (*GACH-I-KUSHTA*)

The dead burned fraction of the gypsum is used for this low strength plaster, which can be used as filler on wall surfaces before applying a coat of paint. Preparation and use is similar to the preparation of wet gypsum mix, but as hardening is slower it is possible if necessary to add some water during the work to soften the mix for easy application. ▪

Figure 9.9: Ghurid plaster wall decoration and inscription (Quran verses) at the southern iwan of the Friday mosque. Photo: Najimi, 2013.

Figure 10.1: The minaret of Jam in Ghur province, after retaining walls along the river and preservation work at its base has been implemented. Photo: J. Leslie, 2013.

CHAPTER 10

CONTINUED CONSERVATION OF CULTURAL HERITAGE IN AFGHANISTAN

WITH FOCUS ON GHUR AND HERAT

While the main account in this book has been focused on the restoration work of the Ghurid Portal of the Friday Mosque of Herat, Afghanistan, undertaken fifty years ago, this chapter provides details also about preserving the cultural heritage in Ghur and Herat in the aftermath.

Afghanistan was an attraction both for individual tourists, scholars, archaeologists and also oriental institutes especially during the 1960s and 1970s. While archaeologists belonging to different international institutions were studying the ancient sites in Afghanistan, some initiatives also resulted in the restoration of the historical monuments. We mentioned earlier in this book that architect A. Lézine working on the restoration of a Buddhist Stupa in Guldara, south of Kabul, in 1962-63, and architect Andrea Bruno restoring the mausoleum of Abdul-Razaq in Ghazni in 1960, followed by the Afghan National museum undertaking of conservation works of the twelfth-century Ghurid portal at the Friday Mosque of Herat, by Erik Hansen and his team in 1964. Here we would like to mention some more initiatives continued in restoration and conservation of cultural heritage and monuments in Afghanistan.

IsMEO (L'Istituto Italiano peril Medio ed Estremo Oriente) carried out the preservation of the Moghul buildings in Bagh-i-Babur historic garden of Kabul i.e. the Babur grave and the Shah-Jahan mosque were restored in 1966. In Herat, the Danish architect Johannes Hertz worked on the stabilization of the main iwan of the Khwaja Abdullah Ansari complex (1967-68). Similarly, R. Sen Gupta and Braj Basi Lal, consultants from the Archaeological Survey of India (ASI), carried out the conservation works on the Buddha statues of Bamiyan in 1968-72. At this period another Danish architect Gilbert Jespersen (assignment by DANIDA in support of UNESCO) worked on a project aimed at diverting surface water drainage from the Bamiyan Buddha cliff that housed the statues. Gupta and Lal also helped the restoration of the dome of the Khwaja Parsa mosque in Balkh in 1968-74. Most of these activities took place under the auspices of the National Museum of Kabul and the Institute of Archaeology of Afghanistan.

The Department for Protection of Historic Monuments (DoHM), within the structure of the Ministry of Information and Culture, was established in 1975, when the Afghan government at the same year initiated restoration of the historic Citadel of Herat's Old City with help of UNESCO. The government, for the first time, employed university students of architecture to undertake a survey of the historic monuments in the Old City and the province of Herat; followed by the employment of graduate architects and structural engineers as staff of DoHM. Along the Italian team, under supervision of Architect Andrea Bruno, the Danish architect Flemming Aalund (assignment by DANIDA in support of UNESCO), participated in the project of the Citadel and the Timurid Minarets of Herat in 1977-78. While some conservation activity progressed well, these works, unfortunately, were stopped in 1979, as the political conflict and instability in the country intensified. To a limited degree, some work was continued by DoHM during the 1980s, a number of Afghan artists, archaeologists and researchers based in Herat pursued their limited efforts on a few sites close to the city i.e. the Friday Mosque (Masjid-i-Jami), the cistern of Char Suq, the citadel, Gazergah, the Timurid minarets (the Musallah site) (Tirard-Collet, 1998). Sayed Azim Reha, Haji Abdul Ahad, Haji Abubakr were among the few based in the Friday Mosque office of DoHM, supervising the tile workshop, as well as the repair and maintenance of the tile panels at the Friday Mosque and the Gazergah complex. Elderly masons, like Khalifa Ahmad and others, were the masters of Arch and dome constructions.

The war in Afghanistan has unfortunately worked against all these efforts for conservation. Historic buildings mainly in Herat were at times intentionally targeted and systematically bombarded; some were shot at by heavy artillery during the 1980s, to reduce the morale of the inhabitants opposing the ruling regime. The 27 meter high, ribbed dome of the mausoleum of Gowharshad, was struck by Soviet shells in autumn 1985. In the same year one of the minarets fell down and other minarets got severe bullets holes. The mausoleum of Toman-Agha (known as the Gowharshad of Kohsan – west of Herat), Abul-Walid, Houz-i-Karbas, and many more were badly damaged or destroyed. (Tirard-Collet, 1998).

Change of political power at provincial level in Herat was peaceful in 1992, which allowed for operations in mine-clearance followed by working for rehabilitation and reconstruction of the damaged infrastructure. The Danish organization DACAAR participated in the reconstruction of war damaged buildings and the infrastructure of Herat city as of 1993. DACAAR Herat, as it was then called, having the professional capacity, undertook some sizeable stabilization and restoration works on the historic structures in 1993-95. The 15th century mosque of Houz-i-karbas, Gowharshad mausoleum (north of the city), Toman Agha (Gowharshad of Kohsan), Hamams of Zendajan and Shakiban, the community centres of Mahala-i-Babaji, parts of the Friday Mosque of Ziaratjah and the 14th century bridge of Malan were preserved and / or restored (Najimi, 2009).

UNESCO sent an evaluation mission to Jam in 1995, and consequently initiated some protection work against flooding at the base of the minaret that a local villager of Jam implemented in 1996. Surroundings of the site have suffered from the extensive illegal excavations of antiquities after 1995.

RENEWED INTEREST FOR CONSERVATION AFTER 2002

After many years of skirmishes (1978-2001), a new government of Afghanistan was introduced and supported by the UN and USA in 2001. This time it was the alliance of western powers that laid out the policies of governance and provided funding. Along other sectors and reconstruction activities in the country, the preservation of key and visible cultural heritage of Afghanistan also got some attention. The twelfth-century Minaret of Jam in Ghur province was added to the UNESCO list of World Heritage in danger in 2002, the first Afghan site with such recognition. The Bamiyan statues were blasted by the Taliban government in 2001. The cultural landscape and archeological remains of the Bamian valley was added to the list in 2003. The Bamian valley with Buddhist caves became the focus of a much publicized conservation campaign where ICOMOS and UNESCO have been involved in making studies and plans after 2003 and still continues. The Bamiyan valley was added to the World Monuments Watch List of Most Endangered Sites in 2008. UNESCO's "Expert Working Group Meeting on the Safeguarding of the Cultural Landscape and Archaeological Remains of the Bamiyan Valley of Afghanistan" had its 12th meeting in 2013. Herat and Jam are also normally discussed in these meetings.

The Aga Khan Trust for Culture (AKTC), through its Historic City Support Program (HCSP) has been another major organization working in preservation of Afghan cultural heritage since 2002. After having preserved a number of buildings in the Old City of Kabul, AKTC carried out restoration works in Herat in 2005-10. Herat city being the capital of at least two major dynasties, the twelfth-century Ghurids and the fifteenth-century Timurids, has still had manifested a glorious collection of built civilization. The buildings of water cisterns of Chaharsuq and the Malik (cistern and mosque complex) were restored and became spaces for cultural activities. A number of historic houses were stabilized and main pedestrian streets in the Old City quarter of Bardurani were improved by pavements using local building material. Conservation of the fifteenth-century citadel of Herat, the Qala-i-Ikhtyarrudin, was an additional conservation project undertaken by AKTC (2009-11), turning the citadel into a cultural site and securing spaces for Herat's museum and historic archives. Outside the Old City, at Gazargah village, AKTC worked on the conservation of the fifteenth-century building of Abdullah Ansari's complex. Similarly, the pavilion of Namakdan was restored and the garden around it was revived. Surviving buildings of a couple of Jewish Synagogues destroyed by the war were restored and the spaces were used as schools. (www.Akdn.org)

Natural decay of the monuments, lack of common awareness and lack of professional capacity with the authorities still pose a threat to the rich cultural heritage of Ghur and Herat among other monuments in Afghanistan. Conservation and safeguarding of monuments will remain a challenge for the future. This also poses challenges to the Department of Historic Monuments, National Museum and the Institute of Archaeology who need to enhance their technical capacity and bring about a better coordination in favour of the conservation of the monuments and cultural heritage. This gap is slightly filled in by a few non-governmental organizations, and the conservation and restoration initiatives being implemented in Balkh, Bamiyan, Ghazni, Herat, and Kabul demonstrate both the need and the potential of such initiatives. The stakeholders, however, need to interact with the communities and the Afghan young professionals to ensure enhancement of the knowledge, recognition and appreciation of value and importance of safeguarding the cultural heritage of Afghanistan. Currently the students of architecture at Kabul University are receiving education in conservation and restauration by A.W. Najimi. He uses an ongoing restoration project in Kabul city as a working case for the students.

It is also necessary not to overlook the need for periodic inspections, safeguarding and maintenance of the restored monuments.

As the conclusive paragraph to this book we can state that the restoration work of the Ghurid portal of the Friday Mosque of Herat undertaken in 1964 has been a good example of a sustainable conservation, which has survived well for the last fifty years. This monument will hopefully stay as a good example for future conservation students. Authenticity, integrity and sustainability, as the ICOMOS values in architectural conservation process, are very well visible.

Ghurid and thereafter the Timurid decorative elements exhibit the 12th and then 15th century's architectures ornamental techniques and workmanship that have been source of inspiration for many studies and research. The Ghurid portal is a unique Ghurid architecture that also exhibit historic work by Timurids. ▪

Figure 10.2: The restored Ghurid portal has now survived for 50 years. Photo: Najimi, 2013.

CONCLUSION

We can conclude this book by stating that the Ghurid Portal at the Friday Mosque of Herat together with the minaret in Jam are the best preserved examples of the Ghurid architecture with construction in bricks and the application of geometric patterns from carefully prepared terracotta elements and decorative carvings in plaster. It is also important to recognize that this was the first building in Herat that was decorated with bricks glazed in turquoise blue.

Figure 10.3: The upper part of the Ghurid portal, seen from the roof of the Friday mosque of Herat. Photo: Jolyon Leslie 2013.

Looking at it from the conservation point of view, it is interesting that the Timurid authorities recognized the Ghurid Portal as a monument and did not destroy its deteriorated structure but actually preserved it in their own way and clad it with decoration of the time –the glazed tiles in four colours. Art and techniques of construction in bricks, decoration in terracotta and glazed tiles belonging to two different powerful dynasties in the territory, today known as Afghanistan, are demonstrated in the monument of the Ghurid Portal at the Friday Mosque of Herat.

This book describes the conservation of the Ghurid portal carried out by Erik Hansen and the young Afghan team 50 years ago and puts the work in a geographical, historical and technical context. The work done is of a qualified standard, meeting the Venice Charter for the Conservation and Restoration of Monuments and Sites, 31 May 1964, although the charter was not yet known to the team at the time of the work. Today the International Council on Monuments and Sites (ICOMOS) and UNESCO have adopted the charter as the international charter for conservation. ▪

A.W. Najimi
Claus Christensen

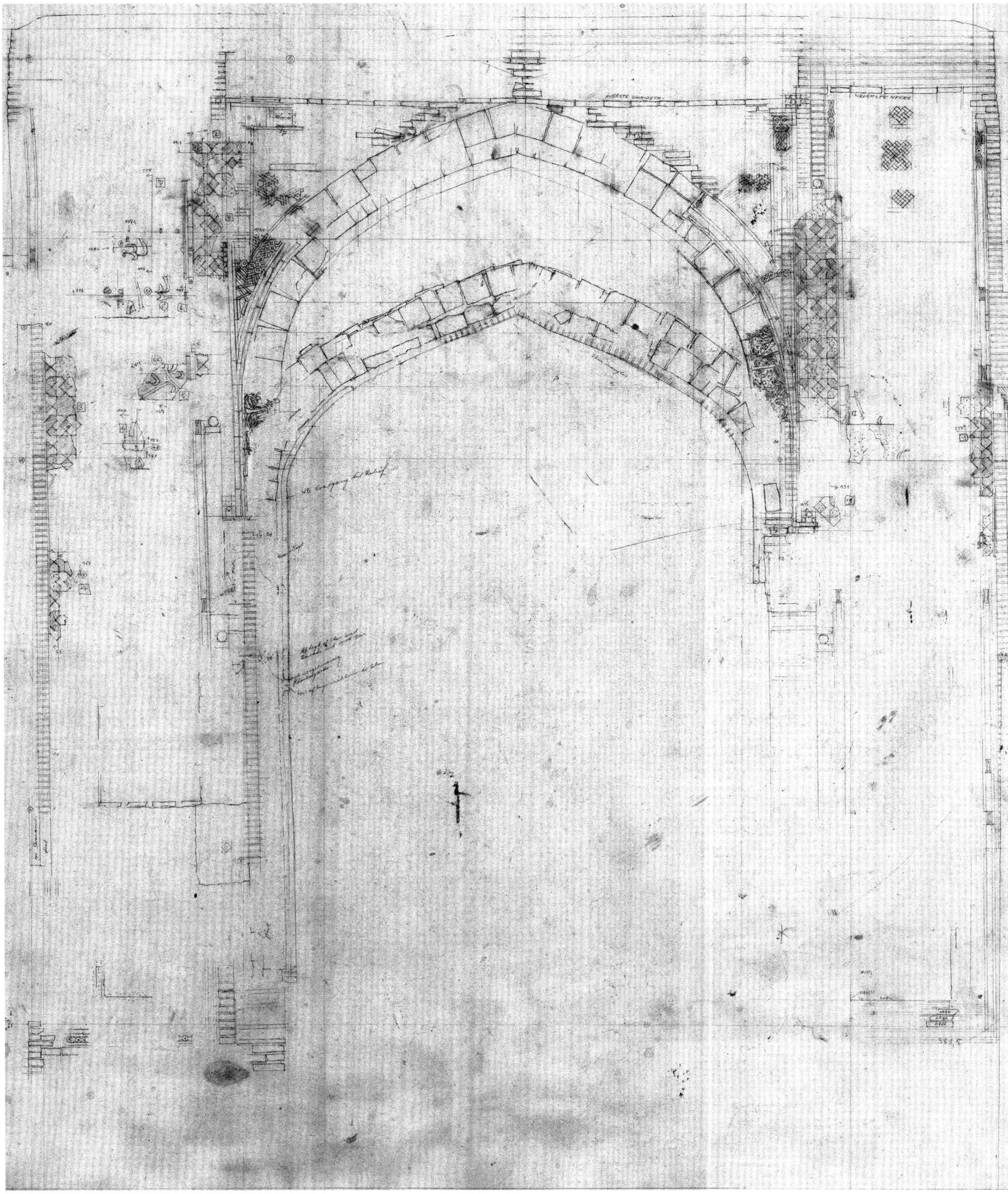

RECONSTRUCTIONS

As an appendix to this book, Najimi found it appropriate to add some further information to help the reader imagine how the Ghurid Portal of the Friday Mosque had looked originally.

Najimi refers to the drawings and the photographs made by Erik and Kickan Hansen: The field drawing of the pre-restoration facade in 1964 (figures A.1 and A.2), the pencil drawing, recording the inscription after being revealed (figure 3.6), the photograph of post-restoration of the portal (figure 3.1) and the details of decorative sketches discussed in chapter seven were used to draw figure A.4.

Also using previous accounts and publications listed in the bibliography and by comparison with other Ghurid monuments Najimi ventured to draw a complete façade of the portal as he supposes the Ghurids made it.

THE GHURID STRUCTURE

In the upper right corner of figure A.2 it can be seen (marked by an arrow) that the terracotta edge decoration ended here vertically but continued horizontally on the façade. This is also clearly visible on figure 3.1 and 3.6.

The inscription and its framing details on the right and left façade pillars of the portal were recorded when it was cleaned and preserved during the restoration in 1964 (figure 3.6 and that marked blue in figure A.4). The inscription on the top were missing. We assume that the inscription was arranged continuously and similarly to the facade of the contemporary monument known as Ziyrat Baba Hatam in Balkh province (figure A.3) and aligned with the horizontal terracotta edge framing.

We allow ourselves, as discussed in chapter three to assume that the text continued horizontally and adjacent to this edge, with letters similar in size and style as seen in the inscriptions on the right and left pillars.

Figure A.1 (opposite page): Erik Hansen's field pencil drawing of the Ghurid portal facade, 1964. Scale: 1:50.

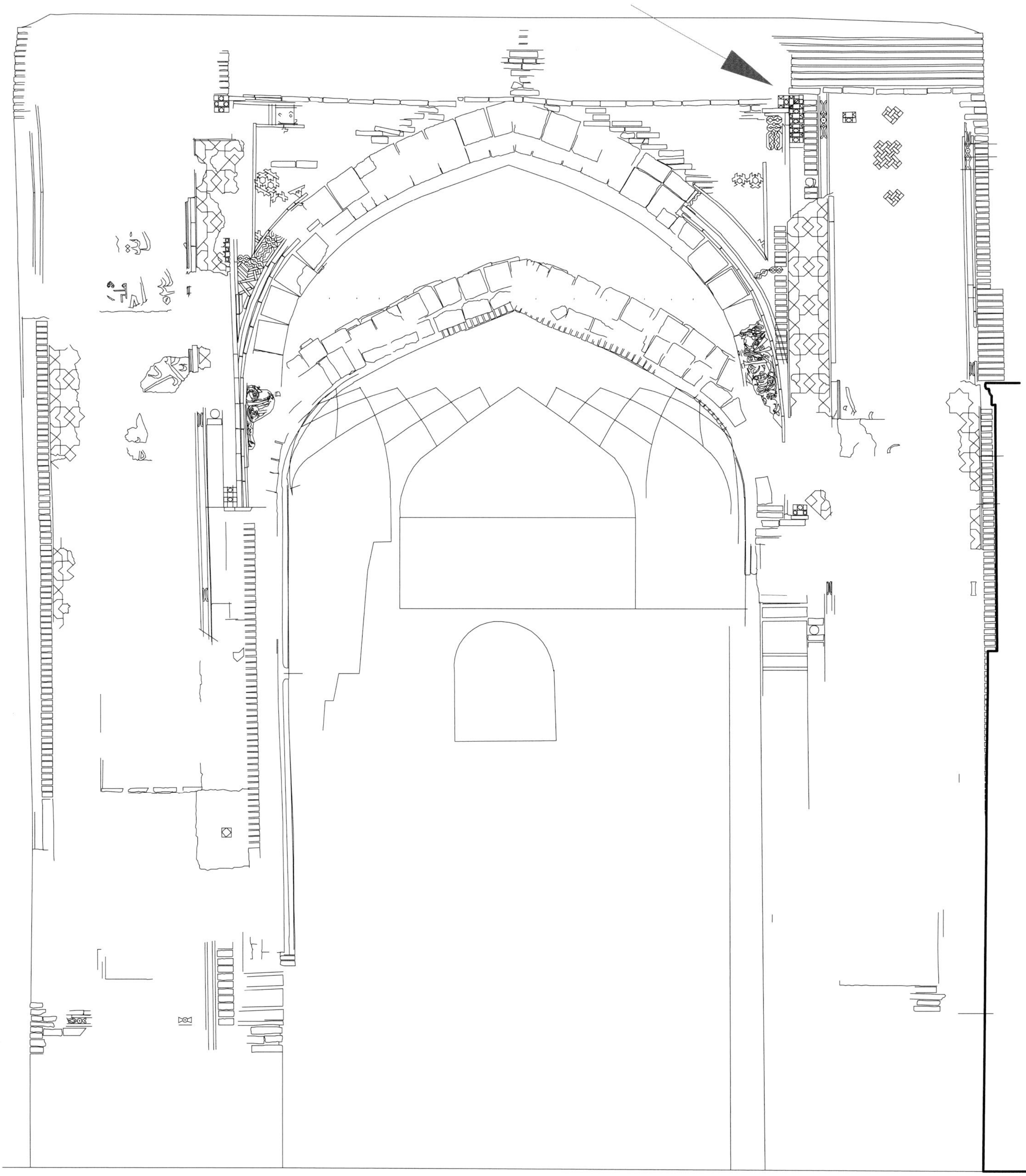

Figure A.3: Façade of Ziurat Baba Hatam, Emam Sahib near Mazar-i-Sharif. Photo: Josephine Powell/Arcnet.org

THE MISSING TEXT

As we do not have any exact record of the missing text, Najimi, not agreeing with the proposed text published by Seljooki (1967) and Rejayee (1982) and mentioned in this book (page 114) with respect to the horizontal space available, has proposed a text adopting the sequence of words reported from the Ghurid inscriptions in the Friday Mosque, the disappeared Ghurid Mausoleum and other Ghurid structures – as listed in the following section. To test its adoptability Najimi used a copy of the same prefabricated three dimensional letters in bricks used in the inscription of the portal recorded in drawings of figure 3.6 to create the upper part of the inscription shown in figure A.4.

Scholars could, for good reason, still disagree with the exact sequence of words adopted for the missing inscription (at the top of the portal) but no word is invented, and the main purpose here is to graphically cast an impression of the portal's geometrical order and volume of the façade as it might have been.

In the following section a number of references to other Ghurid monuments are listed as reference to allow scholars further studies. The general reader may skip this detailed section and continue to the last section: Reconstruction drawing of the Ghurid portal facade.

Figure A.2 (opposite page): Elevation of the Ghurid Portal drawn by Najimi using figure A.1 and photos. Scale 1:100.

THE INSCRIPTIONS ON GHURID MONUMENTS

In pages 114-116, the Ghurid inscriptions from the disappeared mausoleum in Herat are described. In the following we have studied a number of other Ghurid inscriptions in order to form an understanding of the nature and contents of these inscriptions and leading us to adopting what Najimi has text wise and space wise proposed for the missing part.

SHAH-I-MASHHAD

We believe that one of the earliest Ghurid structures surviving is that of Shah-i-Mashhad (figure 1.5). According to Casimir and Glatzer (1971) it was built 561H (1165 C.E). They published the right side of the portal inscription as:

بسم الله الرحمن الرحيم. امرت بينا هذه المدرسه المباركه الملكه المعظمه العالمه ...

Translation: *In the name of God, the clement and merciful, commanded the construction of this madrasa building, the great queen, knowledged, the blessed, exalted, fortunate, wise ...;*
The upper and horizontal part of the portal, where the name of the patron would have been, is missing.

However, Blair (1985) published the dating differently as part of the text of the left side of the portal:

... خلد الله ملكه و ضاعف قدرها بتاريخ شهررمضان سنه احد و سبعين

Translation: *[May God bless] her, extend her dominion and double her power; dated in the month of Ramadan of the year 571H [March-April 1176].*

THE MADRASSA IN CHESHT

The medressah in Chesht had text in praise of the Sultan (testimony to his patronage of the construction) both at its exterior and its interior.

The kufic brick inscription on the exterior of the Ghurid portal in Chesht (figure 7.4) reads:

Right side:
... السلطان المعظم ...
Translation: ... *the great Sultan* ...

Left side:
... بتاريخ ربيع الاخرشهر ...
Translation: ... *(reference to a) date of the fourth month of Hijra year* ...

The gypsum inscription on the interior of the Ghurid portal in Chest (figure 7.21) reads:

Picture to the right:
... امر الدوله الملک المعظم ...
Translation: ... *ordered the great chief* ...

Picture to the left:

... ا لدينا و الدين ركن ...

Translation: ... *of the world and religion and member of* ...

JAM

The minaret of Jam built in 1193-94 has many inscriptions at different levels of its height; all indicate that Sultan Ghyath-ul-din was the patron of construction. According to Maricq-Wiet, 1957, 26 and 27 (Judi, Moline, 1973/74) the glazed inscription was:

السلطان المعظم شاهنشاه الاعظم غياث الدنيا والدين معز الاسلام والمسلمين ابوالفتح
محمد بن سام...قسيم امير المؤمنين خلدالله ملكه

Translation: *the Sultan, the great emperor, legend of the material world and the faith [religion], honour of Islam and the Muslims, Father of conquest Mohammad son of Sam ... Viceroy of the Amir of the faithful, May God protect his territory ...*

This was believed to celebrate the reign of Ghiyath al-din Muhammad ibn Sam who ruled for 40 years (1163-1203). The levels below each have the text as follows:

السلطان المعظم غياث الدنيا والدين ابوالفتح محمد بن سام

Translation: *The magnificent Sultan, legend of the World and of Religion), the Father of Conquest, Muhammad, son of Sam.*

قسيم امير المومنين خلد الله ملكه

Translation: *Viceroy of the Amir of Believers (Muslims), May god protect his kingdom.*

السلطان المعظم غياث الدنيا و الدين ابو الفتح محمد بن سام

Translation: *The magnificent sultan, legend of the World and of Religion), the Father of Conquest, Muhammad, son of Sam.*

A text at the glazed area reads:

عمل على بن امير محمد الله ... غفر له ...

Translation: *work of Ali son of Amir Mohammad, May God forgive and reward him (which indicate the name of the architect).*

QUTB MINAR IN DELHI

The Qutb Minar, a Ghurid structure in Delhi, was somehow a duplicate of the minaret of Jam in Ghur. Qutb Minar built of stones had some similarities in use of inscriptions to the Ghurid buildings in Ghur and Herat. Taqwa, Farzin, and Zoor Mariam (2013) report these inscriptions as follow:

At the **second** stage of the minaret the Quran, sura *al-Hasher* verses 22 and 23 is shown. This was also applied on a wall interior at the Shah-i-Mashhad.

At the **third** stage of the minaret, the name of Sultan Ghyath-ul-din is versed in a long royal statement:

السلطان المعظم شاهنشاه الاعظم مالک رقاب الامم مولی ملوک العرب و العجم
سلطان السلاطین فی العالم غیاث الدنیا و الدین معزالاسلام و المسلمین محی العدل فی
العالمین علاء الدوله القاهره و جلال الامه و الظاهره شهاب الخلافه باسط الاحسان
فی الرافه فی الثقلین ظل الله فی الخافقین الحامی لبلاد الله الراعی لعباد الله محرز
ممالک الدنیا و مظهر کلمه الله هی العلیا ابوالمظفر محمد بن سام قسیم امیرالمومنین
انارالله برهانه.

Translation: *The exalted Sultan, the greatest king of kings, who have followers of nations, master of the territories of the Arabs and non-Arabs**), *the Sultan of Sultans in this world, legend of the world and the religion, honour of Islam and the Muslims, guardian of justice of both worlds, leader of the state and glory of the nation, bright star of the caliphate, extender of charity and clemency, shadow of God on Earth, custodian of God's cities, the protector of God's subjects, protector of God's land and of declaration of God's supremacy, the victorious Muhammad son of Sam, deputy Amir of the Believers, may God illuminate his rule.*

*) Persians and Indians.

At the **fourth** stage of the minaret Quran sura Al-fath (#48) verses 1 to 6 is shown. This sura is also applied in Shah-i-Mashhad and the southern iwan of the Friday Mosque of Herat.

The **fifth** stage of the minaret again has attribution to the Sultan, with slightly different text:

[السلطان المعظم شاهنشاه الاعظم مالک] رقاب الامم مولی ملوک العرب و العجم
اعدل السلاطین فی العالم معز الدنیا و الدین غیا[ث الاسلام و المسلمین] بها الملوک و
السلاطین باسط العدل و الاحسان[فی الثقلین] ظل الله فی الخافقین الراعی لعباد الله
حامی بلاد الله... القائم[بحدود الله المويد من السماء المنصور علی الاعداء[علاء الدوله
القا]هره جلال الامم الباهره فلک المعالی...[ناشر] الويه[النصر] سلطان البر و البحر
محرّز ممالک الدنیا و مظهر کلمه الله هی العلیا اسکندرثانی ابوالمظفر محمدبن سام
خلد الله ملکه و سلطانه و تعالی الله الذی لا اله الا هو عالم الغیب و الشهاده هو
الرحمن الرحیم

Translation: *The exalted Sultan, the greatest king of kings, who have followers of nations, master of the territories of the Arabs and non-Arabs, the most justice of all Sultans, honour of the world and religion, legend of Islam and the Muslims, significance of territories and sultans in fairness and clemency, Shadow of God on Earth administrator of the subjects of God, protector of Gods cities … disciplined on rules of God's revelations, tough on enemies, leader of the state and glory of the glorified nation…publisher of aid, the sultan of continent and ocean protector of land of the world and of declaration of God's supremacy, the second Alexander, the victorious Muhammad son of Sam, may his kingdom and sultanate be protected by God almighty who is the only God, knowledge on invisible and visible and who is the most merciful and beneficent.*

Studying all these Ghurid texts, we find that the wording below is **commonly used in** most of the Ghurid inscriptions, while many other words and adjectives would differ from inscription to inscription and buildings.

السلطان المعظم شاهنشاه الاعظم مالک رقاب الامم مولی ملوک العرب و العجم
معز الدنیا و الدین غیاث الاسلام و المسلمین ابوالمظفر محمد بن سام خلد الله ملکه و سلطانه

Translation: *The exalted Sultan, the greatest king of kings, who have followers of nations, master of the territories of the Arabs and non-Arabs, honour of the world and religion, legend of Islam and the Muslims, the victorious Muhammad son of Sam, may god protect his kingdom and sultanate.*

We find that the word [معز honour] might swap with the word [غیاث legend] and the word ابوالمظفر is synonymous with the world [ابوالفتح father of victory].

THE PORTAL OF THE GHURID MAUSOLEUM IN HERAT

Stuckert (1982) Hellenbrand (2002) and Najimi read [of photos of] the text on the portal facade in Kufic style that was:

السلطان المعظم، شهنشاه الاعظم، مالک رقارب الامم، مولی ملوک العرب والعجم،
میغاث العباد ظل الله فی [الارض] ......

Translation: *The exalted Sultan, the greatest king of kings, who have followers of nations, master of the territories of the Arabs and non-Arabs, legend of God's believers, shadow of God on Earth ...*

R. Byron's photos from the inside of the niche of the Mausoleum's portal show in *thulth* style the text:

السلطان المعظم، شهنشاه الاعظم، مالک رقارب الامم، ...

Translation: *The exalted Sultan, the greatest king of kings, who have followers of nations, master of the territories of the Arabs and non-Arabs ...*

Stuckert's photos show that the horizontal gypsum inscription also writes:

... مولی ملوک العرب والعجم، میغاث العباد ظل الله فی الارض

Translation: *Master of the territories of the Arabs and non-Arabs, legend of Gods servants, shadow of God on Earth.*

We also learn that each Ghurid structure has as part of the inscription name and titles of the patron of construction, what is missing in the Ghurid Portal of the Friday mosque of Herat.

ARCADE OF THE MAIN IWAN OF THE FRIDAY MOSQUE OF HERAT

We studied Seljooki (1964) who refers to Asfazari who in 1579 wrote that the text of the inscription in the mosque was:

کتیبه اول: السلطان المعظم، شهنشاه الاعظم، مالک رقارب الامم، مولی ملوک العرب والعجم، سلطان ارض الله، حافظ بلاد الله، معین خلیفه الله، غیاث الدنیا والدین، معزالاسلام والمسلمین، نظام العالم، ابوالفتح محمد بن سام، قسیم امیرالمؤمنین انار الله برهانه.

Translation: *First text; The exalted Sultan, the greatest king of kings, who have followers of nations, master of the territories of the Arabs and non-Arabs, the Sultan of God's earth, the protector of God's lands, the deputy of the Caliph of. ... He who succours the world and the faith, honour of Islam and the Muslims, ruler of the world, Victorious Muhammad b. Sam, deputy Amir of the Believers, may God illuminate his rule.*

کتیبه دوم: شهر الله المبارک سنه سبع وتسعین وخمسمائه

Translation: *Second text; the holy month of God, year 597 H(1200 C.E.).* (See also page 114).

Seljooki (1964) could not vouch for whether Asfazari's account referred to the inscription in gypsum inside the iwan of the Friday mosque or was it mentioning the inscription on the facade of the Ghurid portal. (See also Stuckert and Chirvani, page 114).

Masood Rejayee (1982), perhaps based on Seljooki's account, suggested that the missing text of the Ghurid Portal (extracting from the text above) was:

... سلطان الارض ،حافظ بلادالله معین خلیفه الله غیاث الدنیا والدین معزالاسلام والمسلمین نظام العالم ابوالفیض محمد بن سام قسیم امیرالمومنین خلدالله ملکه ....

Translation: *... the Sultan of God's earth, the protector of God's lands, the deputy of the Caliph of God, He who succours the world and the faith, honour of Islam and the Muslims, ruler of the world, father of grace, Victorious Muhammad b. Sam, deputy Amir of the Believers, may God protect his rule.*

On the Ghurid Portal itself we find the survived inscription that was retrieved by Erik Hansen's Afghan team of restorers in (1964) (page 57).

The right side:

[امرببناء] هذه المسجد من الخاص ماله السلطان المعظم، شهنشاه الاعظم، مالک رقاب الامم مولی ملوک العرب و العجم ...

Translation: *Ordered the construction of this mosque form his own wealth the exalted Sultan, the greatest king of kings, who have followers of nations, master of the territories of the Arabs and non-Arabs [Persians] ...*

The left side reads:

[خلد] الله سلطانه و اعلی شانه و اعظم برهانه و رفع مکانه تبارک [فی] شهرالله المبارک رمضان سنه سبع و تسعین و خمس مائه

Translation: *May God protects his sultanate, elevate his status, grand his wisdom, and elevate his blessed position, in the holy month of Ramadhan year 597 H.*

The top is missing; and Masood Rejayee's (1982) proposed text could not graphically fit in the space available, unless the style of letters are different or two lines of text in parallel are installed.

Alternative possibility is that not all the wordings found in the inscriptions suggested above were installed on the portal, but something shorter that would highlight the *Sultan's* titles and involvement.

However, studying all the many inscriptions known from Herat to Delhi two things were clear: deputy of khalifa… and victorious Mohammad son of Sam Qasim amir of the believers are in all celebrated inscriptions on Major Ghurid buildings in Herat, Jam and Delhi Qutb minar.

... غياث الدنيا والدين، ...ابوالفتح محمد بن سام، قسيم اميرالمؤمنين ...

Translation: *legend of the world and religion, and father of victory Mohammad son of Sam, deputy of the Amir of believers ...*

Hesitant of making a statement, Najimi believed that the space available on the horizontal band should determine how many words could be placed there. Thus copying the letters from the available inscription he tries to make the missing inscription and check the length with the available space and grammatical relationship with the existing two pieces of inscriptions on the (right and left) pillars.

Najimi reproduced in similar Kufic letters the words below and placed on the reconstruction drawing to test its fitting in the distance available.

ضل الله فى الارض السلطان غياث الدنيا و الدين ابوالفتح محمد بن سام قسيم
اميرالمومنين معين خليفه

Translation: *shadow of God on Earth, the Sultan legend of the world and religion the father of victory Mohammad son of Sam deputy of the Amir of believers.*

This was too long for the space, and therefore one had to omit some words but not loosing the content, alternatively:

معين خليفه الله، السلطان غياث الدنيا و الدين ابوالفتح محمد بن سام قسيم اميرالمومنين
خلد[الله]

Translation: *deputy of the caliph of God, the Sultan legend of the world and religion the father of victory Mohammad son of Sam deputy of the Amir of believers, May God protect ...*

Najimi shared this suggestion with the department of monuments in Herat, and asked consultation of an elder historian [retired] who had worked in that department for many years. No response has arrived yet. And perhaps one day a scholar will come up with the correct information. Ours will remain a suggestion only for the use of graphical reconstruction.

RECONSTRUCTION DRAWING OF GHURID PORTAL FACADE

On the following page the reconstruction drawing is presented (figure A.4). The proposed text has been placed above the arch. The existing text is drawn in blue line.

The entrance opening is suggested in reference to the arcade at the Friday Mosque's inner structure which is believed to be remaining of the Ghurid construction (figure 2.15).

The band marked "Possible Kufic inscription" refers to a similar band, which can be seen on Shah-i-Mashhad. We assume that such an inscription had been removed by the Timurids in order to make a proper base for their arch work. Some remains of the inscription in Thulth was recorded by Erik Hansen (figure 3.16).

Now when we draw the sketch of the graphically reconstructed portal the total inscription is assumed as following:

امرببناء هذه المسجد من الخاص ماله السلطان المعظم، شهنشاه الاعظم، مالک رقاب
الامم مولى ملوک العرب و العجم معين خليفه الله، السلطان غياث الدنيا و الدين
ابوالفتح محمد بن سام قسيم اميرالمومنين خلد الله سلطانه و اعلى شانه و اعظم برهانه
و رفع مكانه تبارک فى شهرالله المبارک رمضان سنه سبع و تسعين و خمس مائه.

Translation: *Ordered the construction of this mosque from his own wealth the exalted Sultan, the greatest king of kings, who have followers of nations, master of the territories of the Arabs and non-Arabs [Persians] the deputy of the caliph of God, the Sultan legend of the world and religion the father of victory Mohammad son of Sam deputy of the Amir of believers, may God protects his sultanate, elevate his status, grand his wisdom, and elevate his blessed position, in the holy month of Ramadhan year 597 H.* ▪

Figure A.4 (opposite page): Reconstruction sketch of the Ghurid Portal with the proposed complete text. The existing letters are marked with blue colour. See figure 3.16 for the Geometric designs in gypsum work inside the portal. Najimi, 2013. Scale 1:50.

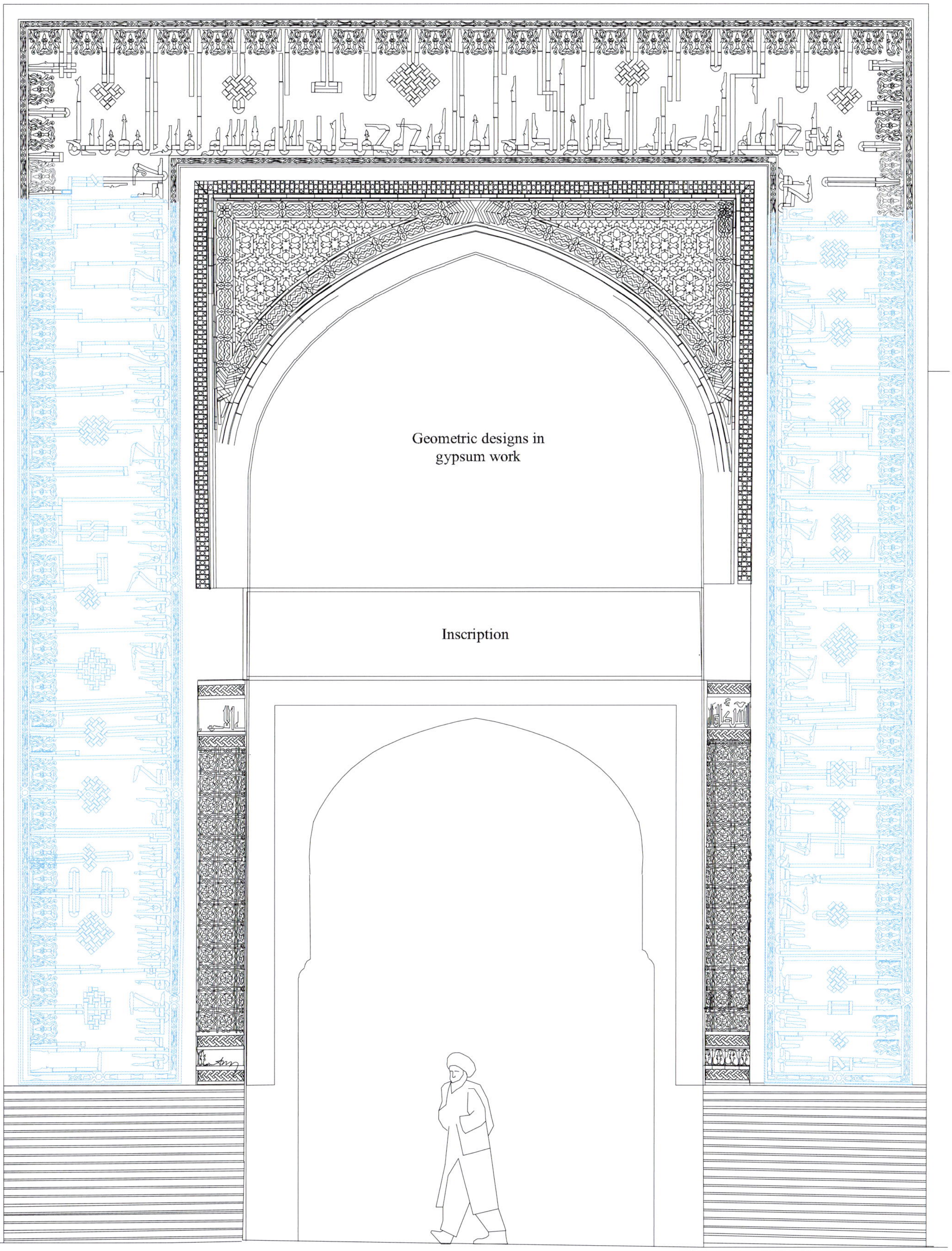
Geometric designs in
gypsum work
Inscription

BIBLIOGRAPHY

Aalund, F. (2003) 'Beyond Afghanistan and Present.' *MUSEUM*, vol. 55, no. 3-4: pp. 62-70.

Aalund, F. (1990) 'Inventory of Historic monuments, Herat Province, Afghanistan.' UNESCO report, file no. 01.

Aalund, F. (1997) 'Vejen via Khorasan og Transoxanien', *En broget buket til Erik Hansen* (Festskrift i anledning af lektor, arkitekt Erik Hansen, memorial volume, article about cultural heritage preservation in Central Asia, Uzbekistan and Afghanistan). Copenhagen: Forlaget Sortedam, 1997, pp. 203-212.

AKTC (2010) 'AKTC newsletter.' (2010): p. 2.

(www.akdn.org/publications/2010_aktc_afghanistan_jan.pdf)

Bjerresø, Henrik (1971) 'Jernstøberier i Afghanistan.' Jordens Folk, *Etnografisk Revy*, no. 4 (1971) (Publication in Danish language).

Ball, Warwick (1982) 'Archaeological Gazetteer of Afghanistan.' *Paris*, vol. 1, entry no. 1023: p. 240.

Blair, S. (1985) 'The Madrassa at Zuzan: Islamic Architecture on the Eastern Iran on the eve of the Mongol invasion', in Oleg Grabar ed., *An Annual on Islamic Art and Architecture* (www.archnet.org)

Bloom, J. (1989) 'Minaret Symbol of Islam', Oxford, p. 157.

Boostani A. and Leslie J. (2007) 'Conservation and Urban Rehabilitation in Herat', in *Urban Conservation and Area Development in Afghanistan*, Aga Khan Trust for Culture (AKTC), pp. 59-69. (www.akdn.org publications/2007_akhcp_afghanistan.pdf)

Bosworth, C.E. (1962) 'Les Ghorides, une grande dynastie nationale' *Afghanistan*, (summer 1962), pp. 46-56; (Fall 1962), pp. 14-25.

Bosworth, C.E. (1961) 'The Early Islamic History of Ghur.' *Central Asiatic Journal*, vol. 5: pp. 116-133.

Bruno A. (1963) 'Notes on the Discovery of Hebrew Inscriptions in the Vicinity of the Minaret of Jam.' *EAST AND WEST*, vol. 14: pp. 206-208.

Bruno, Andrea (1962) 'The Planned and Executed Restoration of some Monuments of Archaeological and Artistic Interest in Afghanistan.' *EAST AND WEST*, vol. XIII.

Bruno, Andrea (1976) 'The Citadel and Minarets of Heart.' UNESCO.

Carboni, S. and Masuya, T. (1993) 'Persian Tiles', The Metropolitan Museum of Art, New York.

Casimir M & Glatzer B. (1971) 'Shah-I Mashad, a recently discovered madrasah of the Ghorid period in Gargistan, Afghanistan'. *EAST AND WEST*, IsMEO, vol. 21, no. 1-2: pp. 53-68.

Casimir, Michael J. and Bernt Glazer (2009) 'The Shah-I-Mashhad Documentation.' *Wissenschaftliche Arbeitsgemeinschaft Afghanistan - AGA Afghanistan Research Group - ARG*

Chirvani, Melikian (1970) 'Eastern Iranian Architecture, Apropos the Ghurid parts of the great mosque of Herat.' *SOAS*, vol. 33, no. 2: pp. 322-327.

Chodzko, Alexander (1980) 'Herat, sa Fondation, sa Position', in *Revue de l'Orient de l'Algérie et des Colonies, nouvelle série, tome 13*, 1956, pp. 281-291.

Christensen, Claus (1972-73) 'Hvordan man gør jern i Afghanistan.' *Støberiet*, no. 10, 11 and 12 (1973) and no. 1 (1972) (Publication in Danish language).

Cromwell, P.R. (2009) 'The Search for Quasi-Periodicity in Islamic 5-fold Ornament.' *Mathematical Intelligencer,* vol. 31, no. 1: pp. 36–56.

Dhamija, Ram 1975, 'Use of Brick and Tile in Persian Islamic Architecture.' *India International Centre Quarterly,* vol. 2, no. 3, (1975): pp. 218-220.

Dupree, L. (1980) 'Afghanistan', USA.

English , Paul (1973) 'The Traditional City of Herat, Afghanistan' in Carl Brown ed. *From Madina to Metropolis,* pp 73-93.

Ettinghausen, Richard Grabar, Oleg and Jenkins-Madina, Marilyn (2003), 'Islamic Art and Architecture, 650-1250', New Haven: Yale University Press, 2001, p. 66.

Flood, F B. (2009) 'Objects of Translation: Material Culture and Medieval "Hindu-Muslim" Encounter', Princeton: Princeton University Press. p. 96.

Frye, Richard (1966-69) 'Herat' in *Encyclopedia of Islam,* new edn., pp. 43-44.

Frye, Richard (1948) 'Two Timurid monuments in Herat' in *Atribus Asia II,* pp. 206-212. Glatzer, Bernt (1980) 'Das Mausoleum und die Moschee des Ghoriden Ghiyat-ud-Din in Herat.' *Afghanistan Journal,* vol. 7, no.1: pp. 6-22.

Golombek, L. (1983) 'The resilience of the Friday Mosque: the case of Herat.' *Moqarnas,* vol. XX: pp. 95-102. (www.archnet.org/system/publications/contents/3052/original/ DPC0346.PDF?1384770662).

Golombek, L. & Wilber D.N.(1988) 'The Timurid Architecture of Iran and Turan.' 2 vols., 'Princeton Monographs' in *Art and Archaeology*, vol. XLVI. Princeton, N.J.: Princeton University Press, 1989.

Habibi, Abdul Hai (1968) 'The effect of the Culture of Herat on Asia.' *Afghanistan Quarterly,* (1968): pp. 1-7.

Hansen, Erik (1964) 'Mission reports to UNESCO.'

Herberg, W. (1976) 'Topographische Feldarbeiten in Ghor.' *Afghanistan Journal,* heft 2: pp. 51-69.

Hillenbrand, Robert (2000), 'The architecture of the Ghaznavids and Ghurids', in Carole Hillenbrand, ed., The Sultan's Turret: Studies in Honour of Clifford Edmund Bosworth, Volume 2: Studies in Persian and Turkish Culture, Brill, Leiden.

Hillenbrand, Robert (2002) 'The Ghorid Tomb at Herat', in *Cairo to Kabul*; *Afghan and Islamic studies,* ed. Ball & Harrow, London: Melisende Publishers, pp. 123-143.

Hira Singh (1891) 'Journey into the Ferozkohi Country', P.J.Maitland ed., *ABC* IV, pp. 142-160 Humlum, J. (1959) 'La Géographie de l'Afghanistan', Copenhagen, pp. 146-148.

Jones, Dalu (1978) 'The element of decoration: surface, pattern and light', in George Michelled ed., *Architecture of the Islamic World*, London: Thames and Hudson.

Judi, Moline (1973-74) 'The Minaret Of Ǧām (Afghanistan).' *Kunst des Orients*, vol. 9, H. 1/2, pp. 131-148. Franz Steiner Verlag. (www.jstor.org/stable/20752444)

Juzjani, 'Uthman ibn Siraj al-Din. (1881) *Tabakat-i-Nasiri:* a General History of the Muhammadan Dynasties of Asia, including Hindustan, from A.H. 194 [810 A.D.] to A.H. 658 [1260 A.D.], and the Irruption of the Infidel Mughals into Islam, (Tr. H.G. Raverty) London: Gilbert & Rivington.

Lee, A.J. (1987) 'Islamic Star Patterns.' *Muqarnas,* vol. 4: pp. 182-197.

Léziene, A. (1964) 'Afghanistan: Conservation et Restauration des Monuments Historiques.' UNESCO.

Léziene, A. (1963-4). 'HÉRAT: Notes de voyage', in *Bulletin d'études orientales,* T. 18, pp. 127-145.

Maitland, P.J. ed. (1891), 'Journey into the Ferozkohi Country', *ABC* IV, pp. 142-160. Maheronnaqsh, Mahmud (2002) 'The Iranian Heritage of Brickwork', Tehran: Soroush Press, pp. 408-409.

Maricq, A. & G. Wiet (1959) 'Le Minaret de Djam:la Découverte de la Capitale des Sultans Ghorides' (XIIe-XIIIe siècles) Paris: *Délégation archéologique Française en Afghanistan.*

Najimi, A.W. (2011) 'Built heritage in Afghanistan: threats, challenges and conservation.' *International Journal of Environmental Studies,* vol. 68, issue 3: pp. 343-361.

Najimi, A.W. (2009) 'The Ghalwar Mosque and Girls School'. A project recently re-examined. Danish contribution in post-war conservation of Afghanistan heritage in Herat, 1993-94. *e-conservation magazine*, issue 11, October. (www.e-conservationline.com/content/ view/801/249/).

Najimi, A.W. (2009) 'Capacity building in Architectural conservation in Afghanistan.' Paper submitted to a conference at the Université Mentouri Constantine, Algeria. (www.umc.edu.dz/vf/ images/patrimoine/axel/NAJIMI-ARTICLE.pdf).

Najimi, A.W. (1995) 'JAM', a mission report to UNESCO.

Najimi, A.W. (1988) 'Herat: the Islamic city; a study in urban conservation.' Occasional papers, *Scandinavian Institute for Asian Studies, Copenhagen.* London: Curzon Press.

Najimi. A.W. (1982) 'The Cistern of Charsuq: A Safavid building in Herat after 1634.' *Afghanistan Journal,* issue. 2 (1982): pp. 38-41.

Niedermayer, O. V. (1924) 'Afghanistan' (Leipzig). Photographs in 1916-17. Pagachenkove, G.A. (1968) 'Les Monuments peu de l'Architecture Médiévale de l' Afghanistan.' *Afghanistan Quarterly*, vol. XII, no 1: pp. 17-52.

Panahi, Ahmad (2012) 'Application of geometry in brick decoration of Islamic architecture of Iran In Seljuk period.' *Journal of American Science,* vol. 8, no. 6. (www.jofamericanscience.org/journals/am-sci/ am0806/104_6759am0806_814_821.pdf)

Pinder-Wilson, R.. (2001) 'Ghaznavid and Ghurid Minarets.' *Journal of the British Institute of Persian Studies* vol. 39, no. XXXIX, (2001): pp. 155-186.

Pope, A. U. (1936) 'A survey of Persian Art', London / New York.

Rahimi M.H. (1981) trans. 'The tomb of Baba hatim and its restoration.' *Afghanistan Quarterly* vol. 34: pp. 70-88. (11-12th century monument associated with Baba Hatim in Balkh Province. Unsigned article, translated from Dari).

Reindeke, Gisela (1976) 'Genese, Form und Funktion Afghanischer Stadte, Dargestellt am Peispiel von Kandahar, Herat, Mazar-i-Sharif und Jalalabad. Berline'.

Richard Henry (2007) 'Pattern, Cognition and contemplation: Exploring the Geometric Art of Iran.' *Iran Society.*

Samizay, R. (1981) 'Islamic Architecture in Herat', Kabul.

Schlumberger, D. (1978) 'Sourdel-Thomine, J. Lashkari Bazar. Une residence ghaznévide et ghoride.' *Paris,* 3 vols. (1978): p. 143, pls. 126c, 143a-c. and pp. 30-31.

Seljooki, Fekri (1967) 'The complete copy of the ancient inscription of Ghiasuddins Grand Mosque in Herat.' *Afghanistan Quarterly*, no. XXIII: pp. 78-80.

Stukert, Ruedi (1980) 'Der Baubestand der Jasjid-al Jami in Herat 1942/43.' *Afghanistan Journal*, vol. 7, no.1: pp. 3-5.

Subtelny. M.E. (1991) 'A Timurid educational and Charitable foundation; the Ikhlasiyya Complex of Ali Sher Navai in 15th century Herat and its endowment.' *Journal of American Oriental Society*, vol. 111, no. 1: pp. 36-81.

Sourdel-Thomine, J. (2004). 'Le minaret Ghouride de Jam. Un chef d'oeuvre du XIIe siècle.' *Paris: Memoire de l'Academie des Inscriptions et Belles Lettres.*

Thomas, D.C. (2012) 'The ebb and flow of an empire: the Ghūrid polity of central Afghanistan in the twelfth and thirteenth centuries'. A thesis for the degree of Doctor of Philosophy in Archaeology. Melbourne: La Trobe University. (http://afghanculturalheritage.org/4.html).

Thomas, D.C. (2012) 'The Metamorphosis of the Minaret of Djām—from Ghūrid 'Victory Tower' to Symbol of the New Afghanistan and Global Cultural Property.' *Archaeological Review from Cambridge,* vol. 27, no. 2.

Thomas, D.C. and Gascoigne, A., (2007) 'Minaret of Jam Archaeological Project'. (www.arch.cam.ac.uk/'alg1000/mjap/).

Thomas, D.C. (2004) 'Looting, heritage management and archaeological strategies at Jam, Afghanistan.' *Culture Without Context* 14, (2004): pp. 16-20. (www.mcdonald.cam.ac.uk/iarc/culturewithoutcontext/issue14/thomas.htm)

Thomas, D.C. (2007) 'Firuzkuh – the Ghurid summer capital', in A.K. Bennison and A. L. Gascoigne eds., *Cities in the pre-modern Islamic world: the urban impact on religion, state and society*. London: Routledge Curzon.

Trousdale, W. (1976) 'The Homeland of Rustam.' *Afghanistan*, vol. 29, no. 2: pp. 64-71. UNESCO (2000) ed. 'History of Civilizations of Central Asia.' *Paris*, vol. 4.

UNESCO (1981), 'Restoration of Monuments in Herat, Technical Report', UNDP/AFG/75/022. Vercellin, G., (1976) 'The Identifcation of Firuzkuh: a Conclusive Proof.' *EAST AND WEST, vol.* 26: pp. 337-340.

Wannell, B. (2002) 'Echoes in A Landscape – Western Afghanistan in 1989', in *Cairo to Kabul: Afghan and Islamic Studies*, Ball & Harrow, eds. London: Melsende Publishers. pp. 245-246.

Wolf (Dupree) N. H. (1966) 'Herat: a pictorial guide'. Kabul.

Yate, C.E. (1926) 'Inscription Formerly in the Musalla of Herat', in *Journal of the Royal Asiatic Society*. London, pp. 290-294.

Yate, C.E. (1887) 'Notes on the City of Herat', in *Journal of the Royal Asiatic Society of Bengal*, pp. 84-106.

Zestovsky, P.I. (1949) 'Esquisses d'architectur Afghane. Hérat, Kaboul-Hérat'. *Afghanistan*, vol. 4, iiii, *Historical Society of Afghanistan*.

Sources in Persian language

Abbas, Parwiz (1971) 'Ghurian', in *Barrasi Haye Tarikhi*, no. 31, pp. 134-176 (www.noormags.com/view/fa/articlepage/14059/166/text).

Boostani, A. (2013) 'The Friday Mosque of Herat', in *Memary wa Sakhteman*. Tehran, pp. 84-91.

Ghawas, M. Alam (1982) 'Friday Mosque of Herat' *Herat Bastan*, vol. 3, no. 10. Kabul, pp. 46-79.

Ghawas, M. Alam (1982) 'Friday Mosque of Herat' *Herat Bastan*, vol. 3, no. 12. Kabul, pp. 11-21.

Habibi, Abdul Hai (1971) 'A Short history of calligraphy and epigraphy.' *Afghanistan [Dari] Afghanistan Academy*, Kabul.

Habibi, A.H. (1979) 'Notes on the inscription of Shah-i-Mashhad' in *Hunar wa Mardum [Dari]*, no. 173. (www.noormags.com/view/fa/articlepage/228086), pp. 26-35.

Herawi, Mayel (1969) *The Geography of Hafiz Abru, Part of Khurasan* (the quarter of Herat). Tehran.

Jawzjani, Minhaj-ul-Seraj (1864) 'Tabaqat-i-Nasiri', Calcutta: College Press.

Ma'ruf, Attiqullah (1961) 'Ghur and the Ghurids.' (Dari text), *Arianna Magazine*, vol. 219. (www.noormags.com/view/fa/articlepage/650755) pp. 9-16.

Nadem, Said M. Rafiq (2010) 'The Ghorid empire and its characteristics' (Dari) (www.koofi.net/index.php?id=2799).

Rajayee, Masud (1982) 'Rawaq Ghuriha.' (The Ghurid Portal) *Herat Bastan*, vol. 3, no. 3: pp. 34-43.

Rejayee, Masud (1980) 'Buildings by Amir ali Sher Nawayee.' *Herat Bastan*, vol. 1, no. 3: pp. 86-71.

Seljooki, Fekri (2001) 'Resala Mazarat Herat' (Dari), *The Shrines of Herat*, 2001. Seljooki, F. (1964) 'Asfazari's reference to construction of the Friday Mosque of Heart.' *ARIANA*, no. 255: pp. 1-5.

Saifi Herawi (1943) 'Takikh Nama-i-Herat' (the history of Herat by Saif ibn Mohammad ibn Yaqub Saifi Herawi) in M. Zubair ul Sadiqi ed., *Saifi*. Culcutta, India.

Taqwa, A., Farzin, S. Zoor Mariam (2013) 'The Mosque of Qowat-ul-Islam and the Qutub Minar', 'cultural heritage in India' (in Persian) *Subcontinent studies* (*Mutaliat Shebe Qare*), vol 5, no. 17: pp 72-53.

Encyclopaedia

Encyclopaedia Iranica, www.iranicaonline.org Encyclopedia Britannica, www.britannica.com Encyclopedia Iranica online, www.iranicaonline.org

Grove (the) Encyclopedia of Islamic Art & Architecture: Three volume set. vol. 2. Oxford: Oxford University Press. p. 98.

Websites articles

www.heritagecouncil.ie/grants/good-heritage-practice/

www.worldcat.org/title/grove-encyclopedia-of-islamic-art-and-architecture/oclc/232605788 Islamic-art, http://www.islamic-art.org/glossary/NewGlossary.asp?DisplayedChar=7 www.kufic.info/kuficscript.htm

www.unesco.org/culture/museum-for-dialogue/item/en/214/brick-panel-with-insertedstuccotiles

www.uvm.edu/~envprog/madrassah/madrassah-history.pdf www.alamahabibi.com/English%20Articles/ Calligraphy.htm www.cemml.colostate.edu/cultural/09476/afgh05-182.html

ACRONYMS

AKTC	Aga Khan Trust for Culture
DACAAR	Danish Committee for Aid to Afghan Refugees
DANIDA	Danish International Development Agency
ICOMOS	International Council on Monuments and Sites
IsMEO	L'Istituto Italiano peril Medio ed Estremo Oriente
NGO	Non governmental organization
UNESCO	United Nations Educational, Scientific and Cultural Organization

Inger Kickan Hansen, Dr. Motamedi and Erik Hansen having lunch in Chesht on the way to Jam, 1964.

بماند سالها این نظم و ترتیب ز ما هر ذره خاک افتاده جایی
غرض نقشی است کز ما باز ماند که هستی را نمی بینم بقایی
مگر صاحب دلی روزی به رحمت کند در کار درویشان دعایی
سعدی

A poetry from Saadi, the poet of 13th century.
This poem is found on a Timurid tablet of glazed tile
installed in the mosque of Houz-i-Karbas (Ghalwar)
west of Herat Old City. (See also: Najimi, 2009)

For years might stay this work
We might be ashes thrown out
The wish is let this work remain
as we don't see eternity in life
Some day the gracious person, though
might pray for us some blessing